A Pragmatic Future for NAEP

CONTAINING COSTS AND UPDATING TECHNOLOGIES

Panel on Opportunities for the National Assessment of Educational Progress in an Age of AI and Pervasive Computation: A Pragmatic Vision

Committee on National Statistics

Division of Behavioral and Social Sciences and Education

A Consensus Study Report of

The National Academies of
SCIENCES · ENGINEERING · MEDICINE

THE NATIONAL ACADEMIES PRESS
Washington, DC
www.nap.edu

THE NATIONAL ACADEMIES PRESS 500 Fifth Street, NW Washington, DC 20001

This activity was supported by a contract between the National Academy of Sciences and the U.S. Department of Education, under Sponsor Award No. 9199-00-21-C-0002. Support for the work of the Committee on National Statistics is provided by a consortium of federal agencies through a grant from the National Science Foundation, a National Agricultural Statistics Service cooperative agreement, and several individual contracts. Any opinions, findings, conclusions, or recommendations expressed in this publication do not necessarily reflect the views of any organization or agency that provided support for the project.

International Standard Book Number-13: 978-0-309-27532-3
International Standard Book Number-10: 0-309-27532-6
Digital Object Identifier: https://doi.org/10.17226/26427

Additional copies of this publication are available from the National Academies Press, 500 Fifth Street, NW, Keck 360, Washington, DC 20001; (800) 624-6242 or (202) 334-3313; http://www.nap.edu.

Printed in the United States of America

Suggested citation: National Academies of Sciences, Engineering, and Medicine. (2022). *A Pragmatic Future for NAEP: Containing Costs and Updating Technologies*. Washington, DC: The National Academies Press. https://doi.org/10.17226/26427.

The National Academies of

SCIENCES · ENGINEERING · MEDICINE

The **National Academy of Sciences** was established in 1863 by an Act of Congress, signed by President Lincoln, as a private, nongovernmental institution to advise the nation on issues related to science and technology. Members are elected by their peers for outstanding contributions to research. Dr. Marcia McNutt is president.

The **National Academy of Engineering** was established in 1964 under the charter of the National Academy of Sciences to bring the practices of engineering to advising the nation. Members are elected by their peers for extraordinary contributions to engineering. Dr. John L. Anderson is president.

The **National Academy of Medicine** (formerly the Institute of Medicine) was established in 1970 under the charter of the National Academy of Sciences to advise the nation on medical and health issues. Members are elected by their peers for distinguished contributions to medicine and health. Dr. Victor J. Dzau is president.

The three Academies work together as the **National Academies of Sciences, Engineering, and Medicine** to provide independent, objective analysis and advice to the nation and conduct other activities to solve complex problems and inform public policy decisions. The National Academies also encourage education and research, recognize outstanding contributions to knowledge, and increase public understanding in matters of science, engineering, and medicine.

Learn more about the National Academies of Sciences, Engineering, and Medicine at **www.nationalacademies.org**.

PANEL ON OPPORTUNITIES FOR THE NATIONAL ASSESSMENT OF EDUCATIONAL PROGRESS IN AN AGE OF AI AND PERVASIVE COMPUTATION: A PRAGMATIC VISION

KAREN J. MITCHELL (*Chair*), Association of American Medical Colleges (retired)
ISAAC I. BEJAR, Educational Testing Service (retired)
SEAN PATRICK (JACK) BUCKLEY, Roblox, New York, NY
BRIAN GONG, Center for Assessment, Dover, NH
ANDREW D. HO, Harvard Graduate School of Education
STEPHEN LAZER, Questar Assessment Incorporated, Cape May, NJ
SUSAN M. LOTTRIDGE, Cambium Assessment, Inc., Harrisonburg, VA
RICHARD M. LUECHT, School of Education, University of North Carolina at Greensboro
ROCHELLE S. MICHEL, Curriculum Associates, Lawrenceville, NJ
SCOTT NORTON, Council of Chief State School Officers, Baton Rouge, LA
JOHN WHITMER, Federation of American Scientists, Davis, CA

STUART W. ELLIOTT, *Study Director*
JUDITH KOENIG, *Senior Program Officer*
ANTHONY MANN, *Program Associate*

Note: See Appendix B, Disclosure of Unavoidable Conflict of Interest.

COMMITTEE ON NATIONAL STATISTICS

Preface

The National Assessment of Educational Progress (NAEP) has long served an important role in helping educators, policy makers, and the public understand what students in the United States know and can do. It regularly reports on achievement in three grades, doing so with sophisticated sampling and estimation procedures that minimize the amount of testing time and maximize the quality and reliability of the scores. It is known for the integrity of the trend information it provides and for illuminating achievement differences among groups.

The NAEP program recognizes the value of staying current with measurement practices. When the measurement field began relying on new item types, NAEP adapted, figuring out ways to incorporate new approaches into its practices: constructed-response items, performance tasks, hands-on science experiments, and multiformat tasks to measure complex problem-solving skills.

However, NAEP has not kept pace with the measurement field's pursuit of innovative ways to evaluate what students know and can do using artificial intelligence methods. Computer-adaptive testing, automated item generation, and automated scoring are all are rapidly making inroads into K–12 assessment with the promise of increased efficiency and lower costs. At the same time, cost containment has increasingly become an issue for NAEP. While NAEP is a highly respected program and a source of valuable information about America's school children, it is also very expensive. Artificial intelligence and other contemporary methods offer the potential to control costs and increase efficiency, enabling NAEP to continue well into the future.

In this context, the Institute of Education Sciences (IES) of the U.S. Department of Education asked the National Academies of Sciences, Engineering, and Medicine (the National Academies) for advice about ways to maintain NAEP's role as a leader in educational testing without making it cost prohibitive. This report is the response to that request.

The report would not have been possible without the contributions of many people.

On behalf of the panel, I extend our deepest appreciation to the sponsor of this work: without support from IES and staff with the National Center for Education Statistics (NCES), this study would not have come to fruition. In particular, we thank Mark Schneider, director of IES; Peggy Carr, commissioner, and William Tirre, senior technical advisor, at NCES; and the staff in the Assessment Division of NCES, including Gina Broxterman, Jing Chen, Allison Deigan, Enis Dogan, Pat Etienne, Eunice Greer, Shawn Kline, Dan McGrath, Nadia McLaughlin, Eddie Rivers, Holly Spurlock, and Bill Ward. Our colleagues at NCES spent countless hours responding to the panel's questions about different aspects of the NAEP program.

We are grateful to Chair Haley Barbour of the National Assessment Governing Board (NAGB) and the members of NAGB's Executive Committee, who met with members of the panel in August of 2021. In addition, we would like to thank the Governing Board staff, particularly Lesley Muldoon and Matt Stern, who provided the panel with insights about NAGB's role and perspective on a number of issues.

As part of the panel's desire to place NAEP in context, we benefited from information about other testing programs. Andreas Schleicher, at the Organisation for Economic Co-operation and Development (OECD), provided information about the Program for International Student Assessment (PISA). Joyce Zurkowski, of the Colorado Department of Education, provided us with an understanding of Colorado's state assessment program.

In finalizing the draft report, the panel asked for help in fact-checking the sections of the report that described aspects of the NAEP program, as well as other assessments (PISA and the Colorado state assessment program). The individuals noted above who originally provided this information—from IES, NCES, NAGB, OECD, and the Colorado Department of Education—reviewed portions of the text that reflected their input to the panel's work and corrected any inaccuracies. The panel is grateful for this additional assistance.

This Consensus Study Report was reviewed in draft form by individuals chosen for their diverse perspectives and technical expertise. The purpose of this independent review is to provide candid and critical comments that will assist the National Academies in making each published report as sound as possible and to ensure that it meets the institutional standards for quality, objectivity, evidence, and responsiveness to the study charge. The review comments and draft manuscript remain confidential to protect the integrity of the deliberative process.

We thank the following individuals for their review of this report: Sybilla Beckmann, Department of Mathematics, Emeritus, University of Georgia; Matthew Chingos, Education and Data Policy, The Urban Institute; Steven A. Culpepper, Department of Statistics and Beckman Institute for Advanced Science and Technology, University of Illinois at Urbana-Champaign; Kristen Huff, Assessment and Research, Curriculum Associates, MA; Neal Kingston, Achievement and Assessment Institute and Department of Educational Psychology, University of Kansas; Kenneth R. Koedinger, Pittsburgh Science of Learning Center and School of Computer Science, Carnegie Mellon University; P. David Pearson, Graduate School of Education, University of California, Berkeley; Shelley Loving-Ryder, Virginia Department of Education; Mark D. Shermis, Principal, Performance Assessment Analytics, TX; Martha L. Thurlow, National Center for Educational Outcomes, University of Minnesota; David Williamson, Psychometrics, The College Board; Phoebe C. Winter, Independent Consultant, VA; Marcelo Aaron Bonilla Worsley, School of Education and Social Policy, Northwestern University; and Rebecca J. Zwick, Distinguished Presidential Appointee, Educational Testing Service.

Although the reviewers listed above provided many constructive comments and suggestions, they were not asked to endorse the conclusions or recommendations of this report nor did they see the final draft before its release. The review of this report was overseen by Diana C. Pullin, Lynch School of Education and School of Law, Boston College, and Catherine L. Kling, Atkinson Center for Sustainability, Cornell University. They were responsible for making certain that an independent examination of this report was carried out in accordance with the standards of the National Academies and that all review comments were carefully considered. Responsibility for the final content rests entirely with the authoring panel and the National Academies.

The panel also extends its gratitude to members of the staff of the National Academies for their significant contributions to this report. Anthony Mann organized our virtual meetings and guided us through the many administrative procedures. Kirsten Sampson Snyder shepherded the report through the review and production process, and consultant Eugenia Grohman provided her always-sage editorial advice.

Stuart Elliott, study director, and Judy Koenig, senior program officer, masterfully oversaw the design of the study, interviewed experts, recruited the panel, gathered resources and data, and guided the study with intelligence and care. They helped the panel get its bearings, become familiar with parts of the program they did not know, work their way through difficult topics, and focus on the most pressing issues. The panel's work rests on their diligent efforts.

To my colleagues on the panel, it would be an understatement to say that I was inspired by your wisdom and dedication to improving this important marker of the progress of U.S. students. Your deep knowledge, careful thought, and intelligent analysis form the foundation of this report. You gave generously of your expertise and time to ensure that the report represents the panel's consensus findings and recommendations and that it suggests a viable path for NAEP's future. Thank you.

Karen J. Mitchell, *Chair*
Panel on Opportunities for the National Assessment
of Educational Progress in an Age of AI
and Pervasive Computation: A Pragmatic Vision

Contents

Executive Summary[1]

For more than 50 years, the National Assessment of Educational Progress (NAEP) has served as an essential resource that helps educators and policy makers understand important educational outcomes for students in the United States. As the nation's only mechanism for tracking student achievement over time and comparing trends across states and districts, NAEP is invaluable. It is also expensive, costing about $175.2 million per year. Moreover, its costs are rising, which has led to concerns about the program's long-term viability.

The independent National Assessment Governing Board (NAGB) sets policy for NAEP, which is administered by the National Center for Education Statistics (NCES), a part of the Institute of Education Sciences (IES) in the U.S. Department of Education. Given current concerns, IES asked the National Academies of Sciences, Engineering, and Medicine to form an expert panel to recommend innovations to improve the cost effectiveness of NAEP while maintaining or improving its technical quality and the information it provides.

To carry out its task, the panel sought detailed information about NAEP's costs. Despite extensive NCES assistance, however, the panel concluded that there is insufficient information to completely understand NAEP's costs and connect them to key parts of the program.

[1]After a prepublication version of the report was provided to IES, NCES, and NAGB, this section was edited to remove an incomplete comparison with international assessment costs; reflect a broader range of costs related to management, planning, support, and oversight; and revise the description of those costs.

- The panel's first recommendation is that NCES and NAGB should develop clear, consistent, and complete descriptions of current spending on NAEP's major components and use them to ensure that the budget can support any major programmatic decisions (Recommendation 2-1).

The panel then identified a set of innovations to improve NAEP. Some of these involve structural changes related to the assessments included in the program and their frameworks.

- NAGB should give high priority to considering integrating subjects that are now assessed separately, such as reading and writing or science, technology, and engineering literacy (Recommendation 3-3).
- Long-term trend NAEP provides duplicate trend information for reading and mathematics, although it is relatively inexpensive and provides useful complementary information to main NAEP. NCES should prepare a detailed plan and budget for the modernization of long-term trend NAEP to support a joint consideration with Congress and NAGB of its value in comparison with other program priorities (Recommendation 3-1).
- Because the greatest threat to maintaining NAEP's trend line comes from updates to its assessment frameworks, NAGB and NCES should work both independently and collaboratively to achieve smaller and more frequent framework updates (Recommendation 3-2).

Other innovations identified by the panel concern changes to the major assessment components. The most expensive component of NAEP—about 28.6 percent of its budget—is test administration, because of the program's unusual approach to administering the assessment by sending contractor teams and computers to the sampled schools.

- NCES should continue to develop its plan to administer NAEP using local school staff as proctors with online assessment delivery on local school computers, with tailored support for schools with limited resources (Recommendation 5-1).
- Because local administration will involve greater variation across locations, NCES should collect information about local devices and administration conditions, and explore statistical techniques to produce estimates that generalize across those differences (Recommendation 5-2).
- The panel's analysis suggests that full deployment of local administration might save substantially more than NCES currently

estimates. NCES should review its estimates of the potential savings that are possible from local administration (Recommendation 5-3).

Other innovations in NAEP administration have the potential to reduce costs and, in some cases, also improve the program's technical quality or reduce its burden on students and schools.

- NCES should continue its plan to administer NAEP in longer sessions that allow 90 minutes for the testing of cognitive items for each student (Recommendation 6-1).
- NCES should analyze the tradeoff between NAEP's sample sizes and statistical power for detecting policy-relevant differences in performance (Recommendation 6-2).
- NCES should not pursue adaptive testing for NAEP as a way of saving costs, but should continue to investigate its potential to improve the statistical estimates and the test-taking experiences for low-performing students (Recommendation 6-3).
- NCES should not attempt to coordinate NAEP administration with the administration of international tests as a way to reduce costs (Recommendation 6-4).

Program management, planning, support, and oversight costs account for more than 28.7 percent of NAEP's budget, which is large both in absolute terms and as a percentage of NAEP's budget.

- NAGB and NCES should commission an independent audit of the program management and decision-making processes and costs in the NAEP program, with a charge and sufficient access to review the program's costs in detail and propose ways to streamline these processes (Recommendation 10-1).
- NCES should increase the visibility and coherence of NAEP's research activities with an identifiable budget, innovation strategy, and program of activities (Recommendation 10-2).

The item development contract is much larger than is accounted for by item creation and pilot testing.

- The cost and scope of the item development contract should be examined (Recommendation 4-1).
- NAGB and NCES should use more structured processes for item development to both decrease costs and improve quality (Recommendation 4-2).

- NAGB should commission an analysis of the value and cost of different item types (Recommendation 4-3).

Automated scoring would be cost effective for the large NAEP assessments, which could reduce costs by about 0.7 percent of NAEP's budget.

- NCES should continue its work to implement automated scoring (Recommendation 7-1).

The costs of analysis, reporting, and program management account for about 10.0 percent of NAEP's budget.

- A greater percentage of the analysis and reporting budget should be devoted to innovations that will increase the use and understanding of NAEP's data (Recommendation 8-1).

As NCES develops the Next-Gen eNAEP platform for assessment administration, it needs to pay close attention to costs for technology support, which account for about 16.8 percent of NAEP's budget.

- NCES should regularly evaluate software built by other vendors or available in open-source libraries for use in Next-Gen eNAEP (Recommendation 9-1).
- NCES should ensure that there is adequate expertise related to enterprise software development to support and oversee Next-Gen eNAEP development (Recommendation 9-2).
- NCES should seek expert guidance from enterprise application developers and educational technologists about the platform's projected costs (Recommendation 9-3).

1

Introduction

The National Assessment of Educational Progress (NAEP) is a congressionally mandated program administered by the National Center for Education Statistics (NCES) of the Institute of Education Sciences (IES) in the U.S. Department of Education. Policy for NAEP is set by the independent National Assessment Governing Board (NAGB). Known as "The Nation's Report Card," NAEP provides an assessment of what 4th, 8th, and 12th graders in the United States know and can do in reading, mathematics, science, writing, and other academic subjects. For reading and mathematics, NAEP also provides separate measures for 9-, 13-, and 17-year-olds. For over half a century, the NAEP program has been an essential resource that helps educators and policy makers understand important outcomes in U.S. education. NAEP has also played a crucial role in carrying out the policy priorities reflected in the Elementary and Secondary Education Act.

CHARGE TO THE PANEL

To build on NAEP's past successes and ensure its continued leadership and viability into the future, IES asked the Committee on National Statistics of the National Academies of Sciences, Engineering, and Medicine (the National Academies) to consider innovations that have the potential to reduce the program's costs while maintaining or enhancing its technical quality and informative value.[1] The request specifically focused on a set of computer-based innovations that have been successfully used in other large-scale assessments: see Box 1-1 for the full statement of task.

In response to the request from IES, the National Academies formed the Panel on Opportunities for the National Assessment of Educational Progress in an Age of AI and Pervasive Computation: A Pragmatic Vision. The

BOX 1-1
Statement of Task

The National Academies of Sciences, Engineering, and Medicine will appoint an ad hoc panel to consider several innovations that could substantially reduce the cost structure of NAEP while maintaining its technical quality and value in informing the public about education progress. The panel will review the major cost components of NAEP and related assessment programs and consider the following possible changes to the NAEP program: (1) automatic item generation; (2) remote test administration;* (3) computer adaptive testing; and (4) consolidation and elimination of substantive overlaps between NAEP assessments and between NAEP and other assessments, such as the Program for International Student Assessments, the Trends in International Mathematics and Science Study, and the Progress in International Reading Literacy Study. The panel will also solicit and consider suggestions of other major changes that reflect modern methods of assessment and that could substantially reduce NAEP costs while largely preserving its technical quality and informative value. The panel will review relevant research and industry practice to draw conclusions about the likely effects of these potential changes on the cost, technical quality, and informative value of NAEP.

The panel will produce a short and broadly accessible report that summarizes its findings and conclusions about these potential changes to NAEP and recommends potential assessment or programmatic changes and research needed for NAEP to explore innovations while balancing the competing objectives of cost reduction, technical quality, and informative value.

---

* When this project was initially planned, the phrase "remote test administration" in the statement of task was understood by the sponsor and the National Academies to refer to NAEP test administration that would be carried out in local schools without onsite NAEP proctors. However, in the context of the COVID-19 pandemic, the term came to be understood as referring to assessing students in their homes rather than at school; this interpretation was not the intended meaning for the project. To try to avoid confusion, the report generally uses "local administration" to refer to the meaning that was intended in the statement of task.

---

[1]IES concurrently commissioned two other studies from the National Academies. One addresses NCES's portfolio of activities and products, operations, staffing, and use of contractors, focusing on the Center's statistical programs. The second addresses the future of education research at IES, including critical problems where new research is needed; new methods or approaches for conducting research; and new types of research training investments.

panel includes members with expertise in psychometrics and educational measurement, new technology-based assessment approaches, statistics and data science, education policy and research, NAEP, and other large-scale assessment programs. Given the pragmatic nature of the request, the panel membership was designed to focus on experts with knowledge about the use of technology-based approaches in educational contexts rather than artificial intelligence (AI) experts who carry out basic research or who work on AI applications outside of education.

The IES request was accompanied by a sense of urgency from the leaders who are responsible for guiding the NAEP program. NAEP costs have increased substantially over the past two decades. Although these increases have been accompanied by important expansions in the information provided by NAEP, there is a growing sense that the high cost of NAEP is threatening the viability of the program. In this context, the promise offered by digital approaches that could reengineer the process of assessment design, development, administration, and reporting is highly attractive. At the same time, however, the program's leaders are skeptical about past promises of technological benefits that went unfulfilled: this skepticism led to the important caveat in the IES request that the National Academies consider a *pragmatic* vision for innovations in the NAEP program. IES asked for guidance about innovations that have a demonstrated potential to provide improvements in the next few years.

While focusing on the possibility for substantial cost reduction, the IES request highlights the importance of balancing cost reduction with the competing objectives of technical quality and informative value. This set of three objectives closely parallels the 2025 vision of NAGB for the program, which highlights utility, frequency, and efficiency.[2]

The statement of task calls out three specific computer-based innovations—automatic item generation, local test administration,[3] and computer-adaptive testing—that suggest the kinds of promising changes that IES wanted the panel to consider. However, the request also underlines the importance of considering other major changes that might also show a large promise of reducing costs while maintaining the quality and the informative value of the program. The request specifically mentions one such non-technological change, involving the potential elimination of substantive overlaps across assessments. The request also references possible programmatic changes to support innovation, reflecting the importance of considering any concrete changes that might be needed in the structure of the NAEP program or contracting structure to support innovation.

---

[2]See https://www.nagb.gov/content/dam/nagb/en/documents/who-we-are/2020_NAGB-Strategic-Vision_FINAL.pdf.

[3]Described as "remote" test administration in the statement of task.

THE PANEL'S APPROACH

The topics listed for consideration in the statement of task are not new and have been considered for adoption in recent years by many large-scale testing programs, including NAEP. As a result, the panel was designed to include members with expertise about the relevant technological innovations, as well as members with experience in implementing such innovations in other large-scale assessment programs and members with deep knowledge of NAEP itself. In addition to the knowledge and expertise of its members, the panel began its work by soliciting comments on the statement of task from 16 additional experts.

In its work, the panel reviewed key aspects of the research literature about the application of computer technology to assessment and recent experience in other large-scale assessment programs. Most importantly, it also reviewed extensive information about NAEP itself. This information included descriptions of the program's structure, research carried out to consider possible changes in the program, the program's current plans for innovation, and information about the program's costs. The panel received documents provided by NCES, as well as the agency's responses to a series of questions that arose in the course of the panel's work.[4] The NCES materials and responses to the panel questions provided a basis for considering the general promise of the various innovations, including those used in assessment programs other than NAEP.

In developing a way to consider the potential innovations that might be relevant, the panel considered the overall goals of the NAEP program, the sequence of topics addressed during assessment development and validation, and the types of innovations that are being used successfully in other large-scale assessment programs. The panel broadened the list of major innovations to review to include automated scoring and the technological infrastructure necessary to support the full range of assessment program processes, including the program's oversight and management processes. These program processes and underlying infrastructure can be easily forgotten but are nonetheless critical to NAEP's overall costs and efficiency.

As the panel deepened its understanding of the cost structure of NAEP, it became clear that the innovations described in the statement of task would not be sufficient to significantly affect NAEP's high costs. In response to this finding, the panel decided to broaden its approach to consider the

---

[4]The documents and responses received from NCES are available on request from the project's Public Access File, along with the other documents provided by NCES. Many of the citations in this report are to NCES responses to specific numbered questions from the panel, which are available in the Public Access File. Those panel questions are labeled "Q" in the report. The process for obtaining information from a project's Public Access File is provided at the following link: https://www8.nationalacademies.org/pa/information.aspx.

overall structure of NAEP's costs. As a result of this decision to provide a more comprehensive, though still limited, picture of NAEP's costs, there are several topics in the report for which the panel lacks the necessary expertise and data to provide a satisfying analysis of the relevant cost drivers. In these cases, we limit ourselves to a brief discussion of the cost structure as we understand it, a discussion of relevant observations given our expertise related to assessment and technology, and a recommendation for further work by people with more information and appropriate expertise to examine the specific issues we cannot address.

Reports about the use of technology in assessment often focus on the ways technology allows innovative item types or the analysis of detailed process data related to test takers' responses. Given the cost focus of the request to the panel, these innovations offered by technology are addressed only in the context of high-level comments about the information that NAEP provides and the importance of continuing to extend and improve that information. These benefits clearly relate to the three-way tradeoff that the statement of task asks the panel to consider—cost, quality, information—but they do not relate to the project's primary focus on potential cost reductions.

In the course of considering innovations that might reduce costs, the panel concluded that some of them were not promising for cost reduction but were promising for other reasons. In the context of the three-way tradeoff in the statement of task, this means that these innovations are potentially useful for improving the technical quality or the information provided by the program, but not for reducing cost. If the panel had adopted a rigid cost focus for the report, we might have declined to mention these other benefits; instead, we have chosen to briefly discuss them, while noting that they are not promising for cost reduction.

The panel decided not to devote a section of the report to the possibility of saving money by eliminating assessments, although substantive overlap across assessments certainly exists. It is obvious that it is possible to save money on assessments by eliminating them. Assessments could be eliminated by either reducing the frequency of specific NAEP assessments[5] or eliminating an assessment when a specific NAEP assessment overlaps with a specific international assessment.[6] The panel decided to defer to the political processes that have led to a commitment to provide assessment results for a specific range of domains, grade levels, and frequencies. However, within

[5]For example, NAEP's reading and mathematics assessments could be reduced to a 4-year frequency instead of the current 2-year frequency.

[6]For example, NCES support of the Progress in International Reading Literacy Study (PIRLS), which tests reading in 4th graders, could be eliminated as duplicative of NAEP's 4th-grade reading tests, or vice versa.

the overall structure of these commitments, the panel did consider some ways of reconfiguring the current assessment structure to combine assessments in ways that arguably could provide the same (or better) information for policy makers at less cost.

The study's timing during the pandemic highlighted issues in education related to inequities in access across the system, challenges in the use of technology, and the need for more timely and responsive measures of achievement. These issues have been persistent in education, but the pandemic placed the need for continued improvement in stark relief. As appropriate, we comment on these issues in the context of discussing potential innovations.

While acknowledging the many technical questions that must be addressed in assessment, the panel endeavored to respond to the sponsor's request to write a short and broadly accessible report. NAEP has a large and diverse group of stakeholders who are interested in the program's future direction. The key opportunities and constraints that affect that direction can be understood without mastering the details of the various technical issues. Similarly, the key issues with NAEP's cost structure can be broadly understood without reviewing detailed accounting records. The report references the necessary supporting documents but focuses on a set of central arguments about the program that can be understood by NAEP's many stakeholders.

The next chapter provides an overview of NAEP's structure, goals, cost, and administration. Chapter 3 considers two ways that the content and administration of the different NAEP assessments might be reconfigured to save money while providing equivalent or improved information. Chapter 4 addresses item development and the opportunities for potential cost savings, including the possibilities for automated or more structured item generation. Chapters 5 and 6 address the substantial costs related to the administration of NAEP, with Chapter 5 addressing the program's plans to administer NAEP using local proctors and equipment and Chapter 6 offering other potential innovations to reduce administration costs. Chapter 7 discusses scoring and the possibility of reducing costs through automated scoring. Chapter 8 discusses the costs of the analysis and reporting of NAEP results. Chapter 9 describes NAEP's investment in the technology platform, eNAEP, that is essential to NCES's plans to decrease assessment administration costs and is expected to be able to support a number of other technology-based innovations. Chapter 10 describes NAEP's overall program management, planning, support, and oversight costs. Chapter 11 summarizes the report's arguments and recommendations.

2

NAEP Overview: Structure, Goals, and Costs

This chapter describes NAEP's structure and goals and provides an overview of its costs. It distinguishes NAEP's goals from those of other testing programs and connects them to NAEP's distinctive design. The chapter also relates NAEP's design characteristics to its cost structure and budget and compares NAEP's costs with those of other testing programs.

STRUCTURE

For over 50 years, NAEP has provided policy makers, educators, and the public with indicators of America's educational health. NAEP was first authorized in 1969 and has reported student achievement in 10 subject areas: reading, mathematics, science, writing, civics, U.S. history, geography, economics, the arts, and technology and engineering literacy. The assessment has two components, main NAEP and long-term trend NAEP. Main NAEP administers reading and mathematics assessments to students in the 4th and 8th grades every other year and less frequently to students in the 12th grade, as well as other subject assessments. Long-term trend NAEP is usually administered every 4 years and tracks the reading and mathematics achievements of 9-, 13-, and 17-year-olds.

Like the Program for International Student Assessment (PISA) and the Trends in International Mathematics and Science Study (TIMSS), NAEP is a survey. Its goal is to periodically report on the status of student achievement in the United States and to track trends in student achievement over time. NAEP uses complex sampling and analytic technologies to accomplish these goals. NAEP participants are selected through a multistage process that involves sampling geographical units, schools within geographical units, and students within schools. Each NAEP participant takes a small set of questions that are sufficient to contribute to group-level estimates of achievement, but not sufficient to support precise score estimates for individuals.

In other words, by design, NAEP does not report scores for individuals because no individual takes a sufficient number of items to do so. Instead, it reports national-level results and, for reading, mathematics, and some other subjects, it compares results for regions, states, Puerto Rico, and large urban districts. It also reports data for student groups defined by gender, race and ethnicity, English-learner status, disability status, national school lunch program participation, school location, and region of the country.[1] Long-term trend NAEP reports national-level results and compares results for regions. Estimating achievement results for these groups is not simply a matter of aggregating ordinary test scores. Instead, it is a process of using complicated data imputation models to produce a set of plausible values of proficiency for each test taker. Sampling weights are calculated for each participant and used in all analyses so that summary statistics, such as means and percentages, serve as appropriate estimates of the target population quantities.[2]

NAEP tracks achievement over time so that stakeholders can see how student results change. Main NAEP tracks trends going back as far as 1990, with the testing frameworks reviewed and refreshed every 10 years or so. Long-term trend NAEP tracks trends since the 1970s; its test questions have been largely unchanged over several decades, with a substantial update carried out in 2004.[3]

The administration schedule for NAEP is shown in Table 2-1. In a typical 4-year period, NAEP administers about 22 assessments.[4] They are split roughly equally between "state" assessments, with larger samples sufficient

[1]Although NAEP reports results with respect to these different student groups, many of these categories are not part of the sampling frame (NCES, personal communication, December 17, 2021).

[2]Plausible values are proficiency estimates for an individual NAEP respondent, drawn at random from a conditional distribution of potential scale scores for all students in the sample who have similar characteristics and identical patterns of item responses. The plausible values are not test scores for individuals in the usual sense; they are offered only as intermediary computations for calculating summary statistics for groups of students. Plausible values are used to calculate summary statistics for NAEP reports and are available for the use of NAEP data users in secondary analyses of NAEP data. See https://nces.ed.gov/training/datauser/NAEP_04.html?dest=NAEP_04_S0310.html.

[3]The panel's understanding is that the original long-term trend instruments were developed in the 1980s and that there were enough common items for a scale to be fit back into the 1970s. The changes carried out in 2004 are described at https://nces.ed.gov/nationsreportcard/ltt/howdevelop.aspx.

[4]Congress waived administration of NAEP assessments during the pandemic year 2021 and more assessments are scheduled for 2030 than in previous annual administrations.

TABLE 2-1 NAEP Assessment Administration Schedule, 2016–2030

Year	State and Combined Assessments[a]	National Assessments Only
2016		Arts 8
2017	Reading 4, 8 Mathematics 4, 8	Writing 4, 8
2018		Civics 8 Geography 8 Technology and engineering literacy 8 U.S. history 8
2019	Reading 4, 8 Mathematics 4, 8	Reading 12 Mathematics 12 Science 4, 8, 12
2020		Long-term trend reading 9, 13 Long-term trend mathematics 9, 13
2021		
2022	Reading 4, 8 Mathematics 4, 8	Civics 8 U.S. history 8 Long-term trend reading 9 Long-term trend mathematics 9
2023		Long-term trend reading 13 Long-term trend mathematics 13
2024	Reading 4, 8 Mathematics 4, 8	Reading 12 Mathematics 12 Science 8
2025		Long-term trend reading 9, 13, 17 Long-term trend mathematics 9, 13, 17
2026	Reading 4, 8 Mathematics 4, 8	Civics 8 U.S. history 8
2027		
2028	Reading 4, 8, 12 Mathematics 4, 8, 12 Science 4, 8 Technology and engineering literacy 8	
2029		Long-term trend reading 9, 13, 17 Long-term trend mathematics 9, 13, 17
2030	Reading 4, 8 Mathematics 4, 8 Civics 8 Writing 4, 8, 12	Civics 4, 12 U.S. history 4, 8, 12

[a]Includes national assessments and administrations of the Trial Urban District Assessment (TUDA). Some assessments are given with a state sample but without an additional sample to provide estimates for TUDA, which covers 27 large urban districts.
SOURCE: https://www.nagb.gov/about-naep/assessment-schedule.html.

for estimating results for states and large urban districts in addition to the nation as a whole, and "national" assessments with smaller samples sufficient only for national estimates. On average, the schedule shows about 10 state assessments every 4 years, including two rounds of reading and mathematics assessment at grades 4 and 8, where they are required every 2 years, and one round at grade 12. The schedule projects more state assessments in the later period. On average, the schedule shows about 12 national assessments every 4 years: they usually include one round of long-term trend NAEP in reading and mathematics, a total of six assessments across the three ages, as well as various other subjects, often given in only one grade.

The state assessment samples each include roughly 150,000 students and 3,300 schools for each grade for each assessment; the national assessment samples each include roughly 10,000 students and 200 schools.[5] Thus, in an average 4-year period, NAEP administers about 22 assessments to about 1.6 million students in about 35,000 schools, which means that, on average, there are 5.5 assessments annually for 400,000 students in 9,000 schools. Although the figures vary widely across years because of NAEP's biannual cycle for the mandated assessments in reading and mathematics, the annual averages are useful for placing average annual cost figures in context.

NAEP's current structure reflects several important changes over time, which are described in Box 2-1.

DISTINCTIVE GOALS AND PROCESSES

As detailed above, NAEP is not designed to report achievement for individual students or schools. It reports achievement and progress at the national level and, for some subjects, by jurisdiction, school type, and demographic group. This approach distinguishes NAEP from assessments that produce individual scores for student placement, selection, or certification and from assessments that report school scores for accountability purposes. The NAEP program is more like international large-scale assessments, such as TIMSS and PISA, both of which were originally patterned after NAEP but have developed in distinctive ways. NAEP's distinctions and ambitious goals contribute to the costs and complexities of the program.

Goals

One of the best ways to understand NAEP's distinctions is to consider some of the specific goals that NAEP works to meet. Four of them

[5]Information from NCES response to Q70f and NAEP 101 PowerPoint provided by NCES in April 2021. Typical school samples vary somewhat by grade and subject. Whenever possible, assessments are coordinated to reduce costs.

BOX 2-1
Expansion of NAEP

NAEP's first major expansion was in 1990 to include a trial of state NAEP administrations. The initial trial state assessment (TSA) included 37 states, the District of Columbia, and 2 territories. The second trial included approximately 45 jurisdictions. Congress created the National Assessment Governing Board (NAGB) in 1988 as an independent, nonpartisan board to set policy for the program.

Prompted by the data on inclusion rates that became available with the TSA, starting in 1994 there was increased attention on ensuring that students with disabilities and English-language learners were included in the assessments and that appropriate accommodations were provided.*

The next major change came in 2002 after the No Child Left Behind Act (NCLB) mandated state-level participation and biannual administration for the reading and mathematics assessments in grades 4 and 8. It also added a trial assessment program for large urban districts. The initial Trial Urban District Assessment (TUDA) program included six urban districts, and the number of districts increased to 10 in 2003 and 11 in 2005.**

In 2009, an additional seven urban districts were added to the TUDA program (the number of districts voluntarily participating is now 27). At the same time, a pilot assessment of 12th-grade students was added to the state program.

In 2016, NAEP's appropriations included additional funding to transition NAEP from a paper-and-pencil assessment to a digitally based assessment with technology and testing proctors provided by the U.S. Department of Education.

---

*See https://nces.ed.gov/pubs97/97482.pdf.

**See NAGB site for participants as of 2019: https://www.nagb.gov/content/dam/nagb/en/documents/naep/naep-2019-tuda-one-pager.pdf. For a chart showing participants from 2002 (first year) to 2013, see NCES site: https://nces.ed.gov/nationsreportcard/tdw/data_collection/2013/study_tuda_jurisdictions.aspx.

are particularly noteworthy for the purposes of this report: high-fidelity measurement; meaningful comparisons over time; limiting respondents' burdens; and public visibility along with state and local authority.

Goal 1: Measure the Knowledge and Skills of the Nation's Students with High Fidelity

NAEP takes a leading position in assessment of the nation's students in terms of the quality and ambition of its instruments. Measuring student achievement in the most construct-relevant ways has led NAEP's designers to reject limits on measurement modalities with which most programs live. NAEP makes heavy use of innovative performance and constructed-response items to measure students' knowledge and skill, though they require significantly more time to assess than other modalities. For example, in mathematics, the assessment frameworks emphasize complex problem solving, and NAEP items ask students to solve real-world and complex problems to test that kind of knowledge. Similarly, in reading and U.S. history, extended stimuli (introductory texts) are used as the bases for item sets that measure real-world reading and understanding. In science, NAEP uses hands-on experiments to judge how well students engage in the practices of science, and many multiple-choice items are augmented by various types of constructed-response tasks.

Though these items are difficult to construct and require more testing time, they are key to NAEP's purpose and results. Without the need to report individual scores, NAEP has the freedom to cover domains in ways that other tests cannot. Using highly sophisticated statistical models to aggregate and analyze the data and report accurate results, NAEP also provides important models for the art and science of assessment.

Goal 2: Maintain Trends in Ways that Allow Meaningful Comparisons Over Time

NAEP does more than depict performance at a given point in time. It also tracks trends in performance. That is, NAEP is not just about educational achievement; it is also about educational progress. To meet this goal, changes between one assessment administration and the next need to be minimized. Stability in the measurement process is needed.

NAEP has addressed the trend parts of its mission in various ways. As already described, the assessment frameworks for main NAEP have generally remained unchanged for at least a decade.[6] Within a given framework, most assessment items and blocks are used in different years without revision. When changes are made, either to the frameworks or to conditions and approaches to test administration, bridge studies are undertaken. Bridge studies facilitate modest framework changes, allow assessment accommodations, and allow transition from paper-based to computer delivery. This careful approach has enabled NAEP to maintain trend lines for main NAEP that, in many cases, span 30 years. However, the program has broken trend lines when analysts have found that

[6]NAGB's 2018 policy on framework development calls for each framework to be reviewed for potential update at least once every 10 years, though that review might determine in some cases that no update is required. See https://www.nagb.gov/content/dam/nagb/en/documents/policies/framework-development.pdf.

changes in the measures are too large to link new results with the results from older assessments.[7]

For long-term NAEP, as noted above, the trend lines go back to the early 1970s, in part because some items are largely unchanged since their first use.[8] Since these items measure things students were expected to know and be able to do 50 years ago, some of them may be viewed today as less relevant or less complete indicators of educational progress.

Thus, the goal of NAEP to report trends stands in tension with its goal to regularly update its assessments to provide the best current reflection of the domains it covers. This problem will become increasingly intractable in the face of rapid technological change and the instructional changes that may go with it.

Goal 3: Accomplish Goals 1 and 2 While Limiting the Burden on Respondents, Schools, and Taxpayers as Much as Possible

Limiting respondent testing time was a key goal of NAEP in its earliest implementation. Many features of the program were designed to help meet this goal. Because NAEP's focus was on group-level performance, not individual-level performance, the reliability of group-level estimates was key. This feature means that individual students can take small numbers of items without concern about the reliability of short tests, so long as they yield results that can be aggregated into useful group performance distributions: one of the main achievements of NAEP in the early 1980s was the development of the statistical models to do so. This approach has allowed NAEP to use more complex items (see Goal 1, above).

In the original design, there were several reasons to limit student testing time. The program was originally voluntary. Testing students for an hour or less was a way to encourage participation. Short student sessions also reduced the risk that students' fatigue would overly influence their performance. However, there are clearly drawbacks with the short testing times, not the least of which is the limitation of testing to a single subject, which both increases cost and limits any analysis of relationships across subjects. At various times between 1990 and 2010, longer testing was considered

[7]Trend lines have also sometimes been broken with new frameworks for policy reasons, with the decision not to attempt bridge studies to continue the existing trend line because of change in the construct brought by the new framework. This was done in 2005 for grade 12 mathematics, in 2009 for science for grades 4, 8, and 12, and in 2011 in writing for grades 4, 8, and 12 (NAGB, personal communication, December 16 and 18, 2021).

[8]The long-term NAEP assessment was changed in 2004 to remove the domains of science and writing as assessed domains and replace outdated material in reading and mathematics (NCES personal communication, December 17, 2021); also see https://nces.ed.gov/nationsreportcard/ltt/bridge_study.aspx.

but was rejected because of concerns about student burden, fatigue, and possible context effects if students took assessments in multiple subjects.

In addition to consideration of student testing time, the program prioritized efforts to limit the burden on school staff. Thus, all data collections prior to 1990 were managed by contractor-hired proctors. In the first decade of the trial state assessment program (the 1990s), school staff served as proctors. However, when NCLB mandated state participation, the state assessments were given by paid staff, as had always been the case for private schools and schools in the national samples. Similarly, when NAEP transitioned to digitally based assessment, NAEP supplied the computers and other technologies that students needed for it.

The high costs of these approaches work at cross purposes with NAEP's goal to limit taxpayer burden. Minimizing student burden by keeping tests short increases sample sizes and data collection costs. Minimizing school burden by using paid proctors and providing students with needed technologies also increases costs. Thus, NAEP's priorities for limiting student and school burden are at cross purposes with limiting taxpayer costs.

Goal 4: Give Stakeholders and the Public Visibility into the Program and Ensure NAEP Does Not Usurp State and Local Authority

Another important goal for NAEP is less explicitly reflected in NAEP legislation. Because education is largely a state and local matter, federal involvement is seen as a possible intrusion. Such fears of intrusion were enhanced by the expansion of NAEP to the state and district levels.

NAEP has responded to these potential concerns in three ways. First, NAEP neither measures nor is intended to directly influence any state's curricular goals, educational practices, or assessments. NAGB develops NAEP frameworks through a national consensus-building approach among constituencies that are reflected in the board's legally prescribed composition: teachers, principals, legislators, governors, chief state school officers, local education agencies, state and local board members, business representatives, testing experts, curriculum specialists, nonpublic school representatives, and parents. Building consensus for the assessment frameworks among these constituencies requires time and effort.

Second, NAEP opens its development process to many public groups. Participating states get to review test frameworks and assessment materials, as do representatives of academia in assessed fields. This involvement is not solely limited to test content. NAEP stakeholders are involved in discussions around contextual questionnaires, delivery of assessments, changes to testing time, and other key program characteristics.

Third, NAEP invites feedback on its reports from a variety of stakeholders, including subject-related standing committees, state assessment and curriculum specialists, district assessment and curriculum specialists, subject matter specialists, NAGB members and staff, and NCES staff.

Processes

As a result of its open and inclusive approach, the NAEP budget and review processes include a far greater array of expert groups than is common for testing programs. Those groups include[9]

- subject-area framework "visioning" and "development" committees (when frameworks are under development)
- subject-area test development committees
- contextual questionnaire committees
- state item review meetings
- a design and analysis committee
- a validity studies panel
- a state advisory committee (in conjunction with the Council of Chief State School Officers)
- an urban district advisory committee (in conjunction with the Council of Great City Schools)
- technology advisory bodies
- special-purpose panels (such as the one writing this report)

These groups are in addition to NAGB, which by law provides oversight.

COSTS

Analysis of Current Costs

Costs for NAEP have increased substantially since its inception, driven by both program expansions and changes in administration. As described above, program expansions include the mandate for state assessments in 2002, the extension to trial urban districts over several years, and the addition of 12th-grade assessments in 2009. Changes in administration include the decision to use NAEP-supported proctors for the mandated assessments in 2002 and the change from pencil-and-paper testing to digitally based administration in 2017 (though there were earlier isolated efforts with digitally based administration). The inflation-adjusted costs from 2000 through 2021 are shown in Figure 2-1.

[9]After a prepublication version of the report was provided to the Institute of Education Sciences (IES), NCES, and NAGB, this section was edited to add the urban district advisory committee.

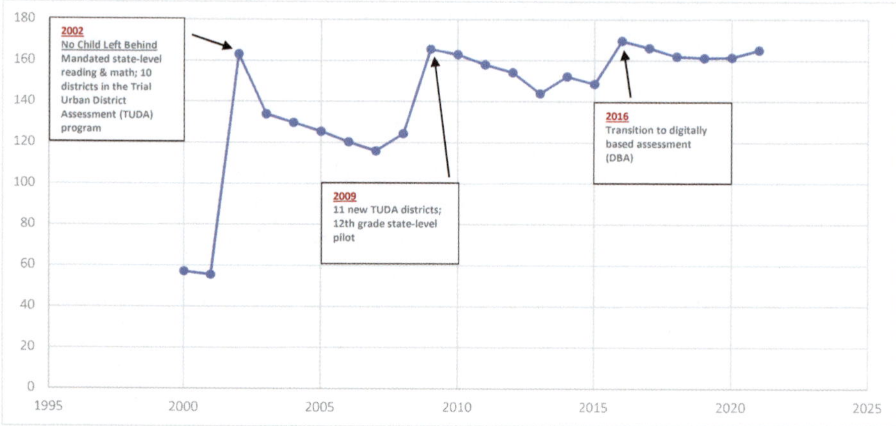

FIGURE 2-1 NAEP appropriations to NCES, 2000–2021, in inflation-adjusted 2021 $ (millions).
NOTE: Figure excludes a fiscal 2021 appropriation of $28 million for COVID-19 mitigation across 2 years.
SOURCE: NCES response to Q51.

Figure 2-1 does not include all NAEP-related costs. In addition to the appropriations to NCES shown in the figure for the operational work of the program, there is also a smaller appropriation to NAGB for costs associated with NAGB's carrying out of its responsibilities, which include board meetings, staff salaries, and framework development ($7.7 million in fiscal 2021). Additionally, there are separate costs for the NCES staff who work on NAEP and are supported by other Department of Education (DoED) appropriations.[10] In total, 32 full-time-equivalent federal staff currently work primarily on NAEP, 20 for NCES and 12 for NAGB.[11]

The majority of the appropriations for NAEP to NCES are used to support a consortium of contractors, often called the NAEP Alliance contracts, with each supporting different program functions. These contracts currently cover a 5-year period, currently from fiscal 2020 to fiscal 2024. NAGB has a smaller number of contracts, covering different support functions and the development of the assessment frameworks and achievement levels.[12]

Table 2-2 shows the panel's best estimate of current average annual costs for NAEP by function, including all funding sources. The cost differences that the panel was able to analyze were generally the ones that relate to NAEP's contract structure, since the costs inside individual contracts often

[10]Information from NCES response to Q50.
[11]Information from NCES response to Q64a.
[12]NCES response to Q63a.

TABLE 2-2 Estimated Current Average Annual Cost for NAEP by Function

Function	Annual Cost ($ millions)	Percentage of Total Budget
Contract: Item Development	16.3	9.3
Contracts: Data Collection; Support and Service Centers	50.2	28.6
Contract: Scoring and Dissemination	8.3	4.8
Contract: Analysis and Reporting	17.6	10.1
Contract: Platform Development	19.2	11.0
Contract: Web	10.2	5.8
Contract: Program Support	6.2	3.5
Contracts: NAEP Support	37.0	21.1
NCES Staff (salaries only)	2.5	1.4
NAGB Contracts	3.1	1.8
NAGB Direct Costs (including staff, office, meetings)	4.6	2.6
Total	175.2	100.0

NOTES: Contract averages for the current period provided by NCES (personal communication, November 1, 2021). NCES staff numbers provided in NCES response to Q64a, with the average salary for DoED employees provided in NCES response to Q64b. NAGB staff and costs for salary and benefits were provided in NCES responses to Q64a and Q64b and NAGB follow-up to Q64b.

reflect proprietary information that could not be provided to the panel. Although the contract structure provides information about some functions, much cannot be determined. For example, the cost for pilot testing new items is spread out across many of the contracts since it includes the separate contracts used to support data collection, scoring, and analysis, in addition to the contract related to item development.[13] Annual averages are given because the costs for many of the specific functions vary by year with the assessment schedule. For the Alliance contracts, the estimates of the annual averages apply the percentage spending anticipated over fiscal 2020–2024, which is the period covered by the current Alliance contracts, to the NCES appropriation of $165 million for fiscal 2021.[14] With this analysis, this report uses $175 million as an approximate annual cost for NAEP. Further details about some of these costs is provided in the relevant chapters.

[13]NCES answers to follow-up questions about evidence-centered design task models and item development costs (personal communication, June 24, 2021).

[14]The appropriations figure of $165 million for fiscal 2021 excludes the additional appropriation of $28 million for COVID-19 mitigation across 2 years. Contract averages for the current period provided by NCES (personal communication, November 1, 2021).

As can be seen from the above text and Table 2-2, it was difficult for the panel to obtain a clear picture of the overall budget for NAEP and how it is spent for the program's different functions. This is perhaps not surprising, given the program's complexity, but it is a hindrance to understanding the cost of the different program functions, comparing them with alternatives, and providing support for changes. Clear and comprehensive cost information is essential as a foundation for the choices that NAGB and NCES make in governing and implementing the program, and as an essential aspect of accountability to Congress and the public.

RECOMMENDATION 2-1: The National Center for Education Statistics and the National Assessment Governing Board should develop clear, consistent, and complete descriptions of current spending on the major components of NAEP, including contract structure, contractual spending, and direct spending on government staff and other costs. These cost descriptions should be used to inform major decisions about the program to ensure that their long-term budgetary impact is supportable.

Despite the limited cost data available and the necessity to use estimates, sufficient data are available for the panel's key conclusions and recommendations. The recommendations related to costs reflect large differences that will not be affected by any uncertainties in the estimates in Table 2-2.

Using these costs and the numbers of assessments, test items, schools, and students tested in an average year (described above), the panel calculated unit costs for NAEP assessments. Table 2-3 provides average unit costs by assessment and student.[15]

Comparing NAEP Costs with Those of Other Testing Programs[16]

NAEP's overall costs are high, but the program's distinctive characteristics make it difficult to find perfect comparators. In addition, the limited

[15]In calculating cost per assessment, it would be possible in principle to distinguish between major and minor assessments with respect to cost, contrasting the "state" assessments with large samples and the "national" assessments with small samples, with the long-term trend assessments also having further reduced item development and fewer items. However, information about these kinds of cost contrasts was not available to the panel (NCES response to Q38). This point was added after a prepublication version of the report was provided to IES, NCES, and NAGB.

[16]After a prepublication version of the report was provided to IES, NCES, and NAGB, this section was edited to note that some costs of the PISA program are paid directly by the individual participating countries. A comparison between NAEP and PISA costs was removed because the panel had inadequate information about the PISA costs paid directly by individual participating countries.

TABLE 2-3 Average Costs for NAEP, Fiscal 2021, by Assessment and per Student

Cost	Fiscal 2021 Cost	Notes
Total	$175.2 million	$165m for NCES and $7.7m for NAGB; omits one-time COVID-19 administration funding; includes NCES staff salaries for NAEP but not other NCES costs for NAEP
Average per Assessment	$31.8 million	Average cost for assessment of one subject in 1 year for one grade; does not distinguish between assessments with small (national) and large (state and urban district) samples
Average per Student	$438	Average overall program costs for one subject and 1 hour

availability of cost data for both NAEP and other assessment programs makes it difficult to provide fair comparisons. However, the panel has used cost data that are publicly available to make some logical comparisons to the NAEP costs shown in Table 2-3.

As indicated above, international tests provide a point of comparison for NAEP's costs. For example, PISA shares with NAEP a focus on group rather than individual scores and an oversight structure that seeks to address the views of multiple stakeholders. PISA assessments are on a 3-year cycle; they cover three core subjects (reading, mathematics, and science) in each 3-year period, along with one innovative domain.[17] Development costs for each 3-year period involve a new framework for one of the core subjects and for the innovative domain.

The international funding provided for oversight, development, analysis, and reporting of PISA for the 2020–2022 period totaled roughly $43 million.[18] Averaged over the four assessments given in a 3-year cycle, the cost is roughly $11 million per assessment. However, this cost cannot be compared directly to the NAEP costs because some important PISA costs are covered by the individual participating countries, including costs for test administration and scoring, as well as some aspects of item development and reporting. Unfortunately, the panel was unable to obtain data on the country level support provided by the 70+ participating countries in the PISA program to provide a complete picture of costs that could be compared with NAEP.

State assessment programs provide a seemingly reasonable comparison for NAEP, given that they assess the same grade levels and similar content,

[17]See https://www.oecd.org/pisa.

[18]NCES response to Q61 describes costs totaling 39 million euros over the period, converted to dollars at current exchange rates on January 27, 2022.

but it is important to remember that their goals are quite different from NAEP's. Unlike NAEP, state programs provide scores for individual students and assess student proficiency in relation to specific state standards. For an available cost comparison, we use the state of Colorado, which has an annual appropriation of $32 million for its state assessment.[19] The state program includes the development of 23 assessments in four core subjects, each of which also has a separately developed alternate version, and then 6 grade span tests for English learners.[20] The state program administers roughly 1.4 million tests each year for Colorado's 880,000 students. Across all 52 assessments developed by the state, the mean budgeted cost per assessment is $615,000. Across all 1.4 million tests administered, the mean budgeted cost per administered assessment is $23.[21] The available cost averages omit various costs that are relevant for NAEP, such as the costs related to framework development and the staffing costs for both overseeing and administering the assessment.[22] Nevertheless, they do allow a rough comparison showing that NAEP is substantially more expensive than state assessment programs. This analysis suggests that there may be room for greater cost effectiveness in NAEP, even while acknowledging that a comparison to a state assessment is not an apples-to-apples comparison.

NAEP's average cost per assessed student can also be compared to the fees students pay to take high-stakes exams, such as the SAT, the American College Test (ACT), the Graduate Record Exam (GRE), the Graduate Management Admission Test (GMAT), the Law School Admission Test, and the Medical College Admission Test (MCAT). In 2021, these fees ranged from $52 to $315 for exams that test students on two to four subjects in sessions that last from 3 hours to more than 6 hours. Individual candidates for some of these tests (GRE, GMAT, MCAT) take exams in expensive brick and mortar test centers, rather than online. There are no publicly available

[19]See https://leg.colorado.gov/sites/default/files/documents/2021A/bills/2021a_edu_act.pdf.

[20]Colorado state assessment program information provided by Joyce Zurkowski, chief assessment officer, Colorado Department of Education, October 22 and December 2, 2021. The program includes English language arts and mathematics in grades 3–11; science in grades 5, 8, and 11; social studies in grades 4 and 7 for one-third of the students; PSAT and SAT in grades 9–11. In addition, alternate assessments for all assessments are given in grades 3–11; accommodated Spanish language arts in grades 3 and 4; and English learner assessments for grades K–12 in six grade spans.

[21]Chingos (2012) finds per-student costs for state assessments under No Child Left Behind ranging between $7 and $114 for the 2007–2012 period.

[22]This point was added after a prepublication version of the report was provided to IES, NCES, and NAGB, to note that the available estimates for state assessment costs omit some costs that are important to the NAEP estimates, such as those for framework development and administration. Despite these omissions on the state estimates—and the resulting lack of comparability between the estimates—the overwhelming difference in costs still allows a comparison to be drawn.

data for the test sponsors' costs to administer these exams, but one can assume that the students' fees for them exceed the costs that sponsors pay to deliver them.

Though these various comparisons are imperfect, they suggest that the costs of the NAEP program are much higher than those of other assessment programs. The remaining chapters discuss different aspects of these costs and possible changes for the efficiency of the program.

3

Possible Structural Changes

There are a variety of ways that NAEP's costs could be lowered if the program reduced the number of assessments or the frequency of administrations. With an average cost of $31.8 million per assessment, a reduction in the number of assessments could clearly save money. However, the panel did not consider the options of simply eliminating subjects or reducing the frequency of assessments as cost saving measures. The statement of task from the Institute of Education Sciences urged the panel to suggest options that would save money without impinging on the valuable information NAEP currently provides to its policy makers and the public. Decisions about when to test, what to test, and who to test are complex and involve many different entities and stakeholders. The panel recognizes that NAEP has existing commitments to provide assessment results for a specific range of domains, grade levels, and frequencies; we decided that remaking those decisions would exceed the statement of task.

There are less intrusive possibilities, however. In this chapter, we propose two types of structural change as possible avenues for decreasing costs but that are more relevant for other goals: the frameworks and their role in measuring trends, and the composition of assessments.

CHANGING THE WAY TRENDS ARE MONITORED AND REPORTED

NAEP assesses trend information for reading and mathematics through both main NAEP and long-term trend NAEP. Main NAEP uses test items that are regularly updated to reflect new educational approaches and contexts. It is the source for trends in reading and mathematics achievement in grades 4, 8, and 12. Long-term trend NAEP uses test items that have been largely unchanged for decades and reports on trends in reading and mathematics achievement for ages 9, 13, and 17.

The intuitive, simple approach to monitoring progress is to offer the same assessment every time to subsequent cohorts of students. Al Beaton captured this in an oft-cited mantra: "When measuring change, do not change the measure." However, his next two lines are equally important, "Precise implementation of this dictum is, of course, impossible in actual practice. In fact, NAEP has modified its measurement instruments by rearranging and reformatting assessment exercises since it began measuring trends" (Beaton, 1990, p. 10). The reasons for minor rearrangements can be technical (minimizing exposure of items, maximizing item information), practical (selecting items to accommodate pages, screens, or modes), or substantive (improving alignment of items to frameworks). Historically, the most fundamental challenges to reporting trends have been framework updates, but even without those updates, it has not been possible to maintain an unbroken trend line even for long-term trend NAEP. Even with unchanging items, the meaning and effective difficulty of those items will evolve over time as educational practices and the larger society change around them.

In particular, the shift toward the use of technology throughout education—and the regular changes that occur in that technology and instruction that uses it—makes it effectively impossible to keep delivery modes the same over time. Giving today's students paper-and-pencil tests will not mean the same thing as it did 20 or even 5 years ago. Similarly, using increasingly dated or unfamiliar technology will result in the same kind of problem. Keeping assessments fixed cannot guarantee trend maintenance when so much else is changing.

Maintaining two programs within NAEP for tracking trends in reading and mathematics achievement is expensive, although the long-term trend assessments are relatively cheap because they use only national-level samples and typically have no costs for item development. Yet maintaining two programs for trend measurement is potentially confusing, particularly when the programs produce two similar but not identical estimates of educational progress. It is therefore reasonable to reevaluate the contribution of long-term trend NAEP to the overall program.

The Case for Reassessing Long-Term Trend NAEP

In 2017, NAGB convened a symposium on options for the future of long-term trend NAEP oriented around a focal paper by a former member of the NAGB, Edward Haertel (2016).[1] At the time, the program was an appealing target for budget cuts due to inadequate funding, waning public attention to its results, outdated content, a lack of state results, and increasing distance from the then-previous administration in 2012. Although the symposium raised important concerns about the program, including its dated items and content,[2] it also provided a constructive rationale for preserving and improving the assessment. Preservation and improvement of long-term trend NAEP are appealing for at least three reasons:

1. The assessment adds 20 years to the trend data available from main NAEP, extending the trend line through the 1970s and 1980s, a period of substantial educational progress and achievement gap closure (NCES, 2013).
2. The assessment measures progress in age-based cohorts (9-, 13-, and 17-year-old students). As age distributions can change within grades over time, age-based cohorts are a useful contrast to main NAEP.
3. The assessment represents a relatively inexpensive reference point for main NAEP trends, which can provide a useful comparison in the event of unusual technical or national circumstances.

As one clear example of the utility of long-term trend NAEP, its most recent administration in 2020 managed to secure results for both 9- and 13-year-old students just before the COVID-19 pandemic closed U.S. schools in March of that year. Now, NAGB has redirected resources to offer the assessment to 9-year-old students again in 2022 and 13-year-old students in 2023. The results will be one of the best estimates available of the cumulative effects of the pandemic on national educational achievement.

Instead of eliminating or even deprioritizing long-term trend NAEP, it could instead be brought "up to code" as the NAGB symposium authors

---

[1]See https://www.nagb.gov/news-and-events/news-releases/2017/2017-long-term-trend-symposium.html.

[2]For example, Ina Mullis noted: "[T]he passages and items in the LTT [long-term trend] reading assessments are unlikely to be considered valid and robust assessments of reading. The LTTs assess straightforward comprehension of short pieces of text that are not authentic in the world of 2017, but are carefully replicated to retain their dated features. Reading comprehension is assessed almost wholly by multiple-choice questions. The LTT assessments will become increasingly irrelevant as students perform greater amounts of their reading online, and reading assessments move into the digital age." Furthermore, in mathematics, she noted: "[T]he LTTs emphasize knowledge and skill much more than problem solving, making them essentially basic skills assessments, with some of the content outdated." See https://www.nagb.gov/content/dam/nagb/en/documents/newsroom/naep-releases/naep-long-term-trend-symposium/Content%20of%20LTT%20Compared%20to%20Main%20NAEP_Ina%20Mullis%20021317_FINAL.pdf.

suggested. This updating could include creation of frameworks that describe the content of the assessments that make clear what long-term trend NAEP measures. Other ideas were offered at the 2017 symposium.[3] If pursued, this effort would need to include a bridge study for transition to a digitally based assessment to minimize cost and increase relevance, as Mullis, Kolstad, and Haertel suggested in the NAGB symposium.[4] In addition, it would be wise to undertake a renaming effort to minimize ongoing confusion between long-term trend and main NAEP and the trend information they provide.

> **RECOMMENDATION 3-1: The National Center for Education Statistics should prepare a detailed plan and budget for the modernization of long-term trend NAEP, including the costs of creating post-hoc assessment frameworks, bridging between paper and digital assessment, maintaining trends, and ongoing costs after the bridge. Congress, the National Assessment Governing Board, and the National Center for Education Statistics should then consider the value of a modernized and continued long-term trend NAEP in comparison with other program priorities. If continued, long-term trend NAEP should be renamed to better distinguish it from the trend data provided by main NAEP.**

Improving the Way Main NAEP Measures Trends

Current policy on framework updates holds that NAGB will review the relevance of assessments and their frameworks for main NAEP at least once every 10 years.[5] Moreover, NAGB can initiate a major update, even as the board is required, in its view, to balance needs for stable reporting of student achievement trends. However, each time frameworks are updated for main NAEP, the stability of its trend measurement is threatened.

Given the importance of trend data in the main NAEP program, the program could benefit from smaller changes to the assessment frameworks that are less likely to break the trend lines. Three changes to the process could encourage needed changes without breaking the trend line, as occurred, for example, with the framework updates for 2009 science and 2011 writing:[6]

---

[3]See https://www.nagb.gov/news-and-events/news-releases/2017/2017-long-term-trend-symposium.html.

[4]NAGB response to Q76. There are currently no frameworks for the long-term trend assessments.

[5]Available https://www.nagb.gov/content/dam/nagb/en/documents/policies/framework-development.pdf.

[6]The frameworks for both of these assessments state that a new trend line will be started, given the change in the conceptualization of the construct (NAGB, personal communication, January 20, 2022). See https://www.nagb.gov/content/dam/nagb/en/documents/publications/frameworks/science/2009-science-framework.pdf; also see https://www.nagb.gov/content/dam/nagb/en/documents/publications/frameworks/writing/2011-writing-framework.pdf.

1. More frequent framework updates—potentially for every administration—could encourage the identification of smaller changes.
2. The use of a standing framework committee with rotating membership—rather than the appointment of a new committee for each framework update—could establish a group with a commitment to continuity and evolution.
3. The work of the framework and item development committees could be better integrated so that content experts and item authors iteratively and seamlessly inform each other's work, with content experts providing feedback to item authors on the intent of the framework and item authors providing feedback to content experts on constraints with the feasibility of items.

Recommendations for standing subject-matter panels date not only to the 2012 report on the future of NAEP (NCES, 2012), but also to the evaluation of NAEP by the National Academy of Education (Glaser, Linn, and Bohrnstedt, 1997). In addition, the recent review of NAEP's achievement levels by the National Academies of Sciences, Engineering, and Medicine (NASEM, 2017) recommended regular reviews and updates of the achievement-level descriptors and their alignment with the frameworks and the assessments themselves. These recommendations remain largely unaddressed,[7] and NAEP's trends have faced threats at regular intervals since, most recently in a proposed revision to the 2026 NAEP reading framework that required substantial revisions of its own to avoid perceived and potential threats to maintaining trend information (Jacobson, 2021). Standing panels with term limits and a rotating structure can help to ensure that NAEP can achieve its titular purpose.

In addition to helping ensure the maintenance of trend lines for main NAEP, the use of standing framework committees to update NAEP's frameworks could also have some cost implications, both by lowering costs associated with protecting trends when proposed framework updates are drastic and by potentially using the existing subject-matter committees to update the frameworks rather than appointing standalone framework update committees. This change would require some institutional innovation—and close collaboration between NAGB and NCES—but the benefit for protecting NAEP trend data could be substantial.

[7]NAGB is conducting studies to review and revise the achievement-level descriptors for reading and mathematics in response to the 2017 recommendations, which were ongoing when this report was being finalized (NAGB, personal communication, March 15, 2022). This point was added after a prepublication version of the report was provided to the Institute of Education Sciences, NCES, and NAGB, which did not acknowledge the ongoing studies.

RECOMMENDATION 3-2: The National Assessment Governing Board (NAGB) and the National Center for Education Statistics (NCES) should work both independently and collaboratively to implement smaller and more frequent framework updates. This work should include consideration of the possibility of broadening the remit of the standing subject-matter committees that already exist to include responsibility for gradual framework updates, participation in item model development, and working directly with both NAGB and NCES.

INTEGRATING ASSESSMENTS FOR SUBJECTS WITH OVERLAPPING CONTENT

Since its beginning, NAEP has assessed subjects separately from one another. Assessments are given in single subjects, such as mathematics and reading, rather than in subjects that might naturally occur in combination. Our statement of task asked us to consider potential cost savings related to "substantive overlaps between NAEP assessments"; the possibility of combining assessments in complementary subject areas is the second way the panel considered interpreting that request, after considering the overlapping trend information in reading and mathematics.

The panel considered several subject pairings. For all of them, we assume that an integrated assessment would allow the reporting of separate subscales for the separate subjects, allowing the separate subject results to continue to be reported where those are relevant.

Current practice in the states is one reasonable proxy to use as an indicator of current perspectives about meaningful groupings of educational subjects.[8] A high-level consideration of trends in state assessment practices suggests three potential subject groupings that might be relevant for NAEP: reading and writing; science and engineering; and history, civics, economics, and geography.

Reading and Writing States are held accountable to the terms of the Every Student Succeeds Act (ESSA), which requires them to administer "a set of high-quality student academic assessments in mathematics, reading or language arts, and science" (ESSA, Sec. 111(b)(2)(A), p. 2).[9] Some states administer reading assessments only, and others administer language arts assessments (often called English language arts), which may include

[8]Some other sources to consider for ideas about potentially meaningful groupings of educational subjects would include international assessments and NAGB's work on postsecondary preparedness.

[9]Available: https://www2.ed.gov/documents/essa-act-of-1965.pdf.

components of reading, writing, and other domains. Most states do not administer standalone tests in reading and writing, as NAEP does.

Science and Engineering ESSA also requires states to assess science at least once in each of three grade spans: 3–5, 6–9, and 10–12. Many states base their science assessment program on the Next Generation Science Standards (NGSS) or a state-developed variation of those standards. Within the NGSS, scientific and engineering practices are intertwined, as noted in the document's executive summary: "Scientific and Engineering Practices and Crosscutting Concepts are designed to be taught in context—not in a vacuum" (cited in Next Generation Science Standards [NGSS] Lead States, 2013, p. 1). In contrast, NAEP has separate assessments of science and what it calls technology and engineering literacy. NAEP's science framework focuses on knowledge and skills in three areas: physical sciences, life sciences, and Earth and space sciences. The framework also lists four practices: "identify science principles, use science principles, use scientific inquiry, and use technological design" (NAGB, 2019a, p. 12). NAEP's engineering technology and engineering literacy assessment focuses on three areas: technology and society; design and systems; and information and communication technology (NAGB, 2018, p. xvii). Some concepts appear in the frameworks for both assessments.[10]

History, Civics, Economics, and Geography These four subjects comprise the broad category of social studies. A recent survey cited in a new NAEP validity studies panel report (O'Malley and Norton, 2022) showed that of the 35 states that responded, at least 18 states assess social studies. Seven of the 35 states reported that they assess all four social studies content areas within one test, while two states test some but not all four areas within one test. In 15 of these states, civics and U.S. history are included in the assessment. Two others have variations across grade levels. NAEP has traditionally assessed all four as separate assessments, though the current assessment schedule shows no plans to assess economics and geography through 2030.[11]

Two other potential subject groupings are not reflected in current state assessment practice as combined assessments but involve substantive relationships across assessments that may be meaningful to reflect in NAEP: reading with science or history, and mathematics and science. NAEP's new reading framework (NAGB, 2021) proposes three subscales that would

---

[10]The NAEP validity studies panel is currently studying these overlapping concepts and the possibility of combining assessments.

[11]See Table 2-1 and https://www.nagb.gov/about-naep/assessment-schedule.html.

report reading performance within and across three disciplinary contexts, including science and social studies. The pairing of mathematics and science is reflected in the Trends in International Mathematics and Science Study.

With respect to potential cost savings from combining assessments the primary opportunities lie with the three subject combinations—language arts, science and engineering, and social studies—that are already reflected in current state assessments. There are several relevant considerations with respect to the net benefit of such combinations: need for new frameworks, assessment schedule, sample size, and preserving subjects.

In all cases, it would be necessary to develop new frameworks as the first step in developing a combined assessment, which has practical implications. Since the reading framework has just been revised, it would not be an opportune time to consider a combined assessment for reading and writing. However, civics and U.S. history are scheduled to have updated frameworks in time for the 2030 assessment, a timing that would potentially allow this combination to be considered.

A coordination of the assessment schedule for two or more subjects with overlapping or complementary content allows for the possibility of increasing coordination across them. This is the case for civics and U.S. history and also for science and technology and engineering literacy. In contrast, economics and geography are no longer on the assessment schedule (through 2030), and writing is not on the schedule until 2030, giving limited opportunities for considering any coordination.

In terms of sample size, the most money would be saved by combining two large assessments that include state and urban district samples because of the possibility of eliminating an assessment with a high cost for test administration to a large sample. However, none of the likely combinations fall into this category. Thus, any potential cost savings would likely relate to the smaller cost savings associated with a reducing an assessment that has only a national-level sample.

The assessment schedule illustrates the cost limitations that force some subjects to be assessed minimally (writing) or not at all (economics and geography). For these subjects, cost savings have been realized by eliminating entire assessments.

NAEP's framework committees are tasked with updating the perspectives on educational goals within individual subjects, and by design, those committees work within the confines of an individual subject. This narrow focus is illustrated by a statement in the new reading framework adopted by NAGB in August 2021 that expressly precludes such consideration: "The 2026 NAEP Reading Assessment will continue NAEP's longstanding focus on reading comprehension, rather than foundational skills or writing" (NAGB, 2021, p. 13).

At various times, NAGB has noted the importance of considering the possibility of assessments that combine several subjects (see, e.g., NAGB, 1996, p. 5; 2017, p. 13; 2019a, p. 7). In addition, as noted above, there is currently some activity focused on considering the possibility of integrating the science and the technology and engineering literacy assessments. However, even the brief review above suggests there might also be strong arguments for integrating other subjects, and we note the integration across disciplinary contexts already reflected in the new reading framework. Such combined assessments could continue to report subscores for the subjects that are currently assessed with separate assessments.

Although there would be upfront investment costs to develop combined assessments, they could result in cost savings from reducing the number of assessments. The cost savings are likely to be small in most cases because at least one of the assessments in each pairing is given infrequently and usually to only a national sample. However, even the small cost savings from reducing these assessments are sufficient to substantially limit their presence in the assessment schedule. One downside of not actively considering the possibility of integrating assessments is illustrated by the cost pressures that force some subjects to be assessed infrequently or to be effectively eliminated.

RECOMMENDATION 3-3: The National Assessment Governing Board should give high priority to consideration of integrating nonmandated subjects that are currently assessed separately (such as science and technology and engineering literacy), as well as the possibility of integrated pairs of subjects that include a mandated subject, such as reading and writing. This consideration should examine the possibility of preserving separate subject subscores in an integrated assessment that could maintain trends, along with potential benefits related to efficiency and cost, closer alignment with student learning, and synergy across subjects that has been found by research.

4

Item Development

This chapter reviews NAEP's costs for item development and then considers two ways to reduce item development costs: automated and structured item development and changing the mix of item types. The pilot administration costs that are a large component of item development costs are partially addressed in the next two chapters, which cover test administration.

CURRENT COSTS

Test item development for NAEP is expensive. The costs for item creation and review range from $1,000 to $2,500 for selected-response items, from $1,500 to $3,500 for constructed-response items, and from $6,000 to $20,000 for scenario-based task items.[1] With a typical distribution across these three types and taking the midpoint of the ranges, average per-item costs for creation and review are about $3,700.[2]

---

[1]NCES response to Q68a. The panel follows NCES in describing cost differences in item development in terms of these three types of items. However, it has been noted that scenario-based tasks are not actually an item type, but are instead a way of grouping and contextualizing a set of items, each of which may require either selected or constructed responses. Thus, the panel's references to the cost associated with "scenario-based task items" should be understood to refer to the cost of items that are developed as part of a contextualized group of items in a scenario-based task that may require either selected or constructed responses.

[2]Taking the midpoint of each range implies an average cost of $1,750 for selected-response items, $2,500 for constructed-response items, and $13,000 for scenario-based items. The NCES response to Q68a suggests the following rough distribution of item types: 45 to 55 percent selected-response items, 30 to 40 percent constructed-response items, and 12 to 17 percent scenario-based items. Using a distribution of 50, 35, and 15 percent, respectively, for

NAEP's item costs are substantially higher than those in other testing programs. Published figures are generally not available, but the few that the panel found and the experience of several of the panel members suggests that typical industry experience for creating, reviewing, and pilot testing items range from hundreds of dollars per item for selected-response or short constructed-response items to less than $3,000 (also see Rudner, 2007). It is not surprising that the more unusual scenario-based task items are more expensive than selected-response or short constructed-response items, but the high cost of the more common item types suggests an unusually high overall cost structure that is separate from NAEP's use of innovative item types.

These costs for NAEP's items do not include the cost of pilot administration to test the items before use, which ranges from $25,000 to $35,000 for selected-response items, from $35,000 to $45,000 for constructed-response items, and from $45,000 to $55,000 for scenario-based task items.[3] Again, with a typical distribution across these three types and taking the midpoint of the ranges, these average per-item costs are roughly $36,500 for pilot administration.[4] These costs are also much higher than piloting testing costs for other assessments (which are addressed in Chapter 5).

Although there is variation across subjects and grades, NAEP assessments include about 200 items, which are typically used across four administrations.[5] Thus, a typical assessment on average will require 50 new items each time it is given. As noted in Chapter 2, NAEP administers roughly 22 assessments in a 4-year period, but 6 of these will be long-term trend NAEP in reading and mathematics, for which no new items are developed. Thus, a 4-year period typically involves developing roughly 50 new items for each of 16 assessments, or 800 items. In addition, sometimes extra items need to be developed, which can be required, for example, when a new framework requires a new type of item or area or content that was not previously covered.[6] Over the next few years, a somewhat higher proportion of new items may be required, if the items in long-term trend NAEP are updated in its transition to digital administration and if the scheduled framework updates

---

the three types of items (roughly the midpoints of the three ranges) produces the weighted average item creation and review cost of $3,700.

[3]These per-item pilot administration costs likely include apportionment of some fixed program costs (such as planning and equipment setup). While these per-item costs serve a useful discussion purpose, readers are cautioned against assuming that addition or removal of items will add or save costs in the full increments suggested by the unit costs.

[4]NCES response to Q68a.

[5]NCES responses to Q11, Q54, and Q55.

[6]NCES response to Q55.

result in new construct demands.[7] NCES suggests an estimated additional 100 items per year to support new frameworks and other special purposes.[8] As a result, the panel estimates that NAEP needs to develop roughly 300 new items per year across all assessments. Finally, it is necessary to develop twice as many new items as needed—roughly 600 items per year—since roughly half of new items are rejected during piloting.[9]

Item development is covered by one contract in the NAEP Alliance.[10] The estimated annual average cost of this contract is $16.3 million, which is 9.3 percent of NAEP's budget.[11] At $3,700 per item, the creation of 600 items per year will cost $2.2 million. In addition, there will be pilot administration costs of roughly $21.9 million. However, only 10 percent of the pilot administration costs are covered in the item development contract, with the remaining costs for piloting new items supported by a variety of other contracts.[12] Thus, the item creation and pilot administration costs attributed to the item development contract are roughly $4.4 million, 2.5 percent of NAEP's budget, and roughly $11.9 million of the item development contract is not reflected in the per-unit costs of developing items.

NCES reports that there are other activities in the item development contract, including "preparation work prior to, during and after operational administration (e.g., Block Assembly), translating assessment content for the Bilingual accommodations and the mathematics Puerto Rico assessment, survey questionnaire development, Alliance-wide collaboration and planning, NAEP Integrated Management Systems (IMS) support, support for Governing Board meetings, and administrative costs."[13] The panel does not understand how these other activities can account for the vast majority of the costs in the item development contract.

---

[7]NCES response to Q66a. The NAGB schedule calls for "new frameworks for mathematics and reading in 2026, science in 2028 and civics, U.S. history and writing in 2030."

[8]NCES response to Q66a.

[9]NCES communication at the panel's June 7, 2021 meeting. Sometimes items are rejected after piloting, but when this happens the item "will remain in the item inventory for revision and potential future pilot." NCES response to Q12. This point was added after a prepublication version of the report was provided to the Institute of Education Sciences, NCES, and NAGB. The correction altered the estimates of item creation and pilot administration costs, as well as the estimates of potential savings to administration costs from local administration and longer testing time. These changes were made throughout the report.

[10]The item development contract covers the following activities: "Develops cognitive items, scoring rubrics and survey questions; assists in the training of scorers; conducts cognitive interviews/small-scale pilots of items, rubrics, and survey questions; translates items and survey questions; and conducts item reviews" (NCES response to Q33).

[11]See Table 2-2 in Chapter 2.

[12]NCES answers to follow-up questions about evidence-centered design task models and item development costs (personal communication, June 24, 2021).

[13]NCES response to Q68g.

RECOMMENDATION 4-1: The National Center for Education Statistics should examine the costs and scope of work in the item development contract that are not directly related to item development and pilot administration and explore possibilities for changes that would reduce costs.

AUTOMATED AND STRUCTURED ITEM DEVELOPMENT

Automatic item generation refers to the use of computer-based algorithms that produce test items or assist in their production (Gierl and Haladyna, 2013; Irvine, 2002).[14] The item generation process involves three steps. In step 1, the content for item generation is identified using design principles, guidelines, and data that highlight the knowledge, skills, and abilities required to solve problems and perform tasks in a specific domain. The content needs to be organized and structured in a logical manner that can promote item generation. In step 2, an item model is developed to specify where the content must be placed to generate new items. In step 3, computer-based algorithms place the content specified in step 1 into the item model developed in step 2 to generate items. Selected-response questions tend to be more suited to automatic item generation than constructed-response questions, and more traditional selected-response questions are more suitable than complex selected-response questions.

Applications in a variety of contexts show that automatic item generation can lead to cost savings in developing traditional selected-response items (Bejar, 2019; Embretson and Kingston, 2018; Irvine, 2014; Kosh et al., 2019). Many of these efforts focus on mathematics items, but some of the work has included such domains as vocabulary or spatial ability.

Although NAEP includes some traditional selected-response items for which automatic item generation might be applied, those items are more prevalent in long-term trend NAEP, where new items are not generally created. Main NAEP, where new items are needed, often uses more complex item types, which are less amenable to automatic item generation. The program's interest in scenario-based tasks further adds to the complexity of items and the resulting difficulties in trying to apply automatic item generation.

The deployment of automatic item generation procedures for a given item type requires a significant effort. It is more likely to lead to cost savings when a small number of item models are expected to be used, and

[14]A term often used in connection with automated item generation is "cloning." However, the term is based on an analogy that is not applicable to test development. A clone, by definition, is a duplicate or exact copy. The goal of automatic item generation is to produce *psychometrically equivalent* items, not exact duplicates.

reused, well into the future, as is the case in K–12 state assessments or in high-stakes admissions or credentialing exams. In an example of the threshold for cost effectiveness, Kosh and colleagues (2019) found that the investment in automatic item generation could be worthwhile within a narrow content area if more than 173–247 items were needed. This number of items is feasible for high-stakes assessments, such as admissions tests, that are administered frequently, and where reducing the exposure of items is necessary for security purposes. It is not feasible for NAEP, which needs only a few items in each narrow content area, though NAEP's cost structure might result in a somewhat different number of items needed for automatic item generation to be cost effective.

Though the current state of the art in automatic item generation has limited applicability to NAEP, there are other options, some of which NCES has been considering. For example, NCES has been using principled approaches, such as evidence-centered design, to systematically lay out the chain of claims and evidence needed to build tasks that elicit the targeted knowledge and skills. The agency is using this approach to create task models for measuring the intended skills. NCES is also creating a library of reusable assessment components as part of its Benchmark Design System with hopes for operational use in the 2024 assessment. The reusable components will provide the building blocks and guidelines for generating new items and tasks.[15]

NCES could push this work further by applying some additional assessment design and engineering principles. Among them are the ideas of drawing from the detailed achievement-level descriptions to specify intended inferences and claims; better integrating the work of the experts who create NAEP frameworks with the experts who write items (as noted in Chapter 3); and applying many of the quality control processes to standardized item models instead of individual items to reduce review and pilot testing costs. We explain each below.

Drawing from Detailed Achievement-Level Descriptions As described above, a principled approach begins by laying out the intended claims and inferences to be based on assessment results. The intended claims and inferences are then recast in terms of the types of evidence needed to support them. NAEP currently has two versions of achievement-level descriptions: a brief one- or two-sentence version that is typically reported with assessment results (and that most users are familiar with) and a longer, more detailed one that is used in test development. The longer version provides the kind of information needed for a principled approach since it specifies

[15]NCES response to question related to evidence-centered design (personal communication, June 24, 2021).

what students should know and be able to do at each of the tested grade levels in each subject area. The descriptions reflect a progression from basic performance to advanced performance for each grade. They are intended to be cumulative within grade and coherent across grades. The evidence claims can then be used to outline the scope of knowledge and skills to be elicited from students at each achievement level.[16]

Integrating Framework Development and Item Creation As described in Chapter 3 and recommended by other experts (e.g., Glaser, Linn, and Bohrnstedt, 1997; NCES, 2012), the content experts who create the assessment frameworks and the test development experts who write items have a great deal to offer each other. Working together and iteratively, the item developers can bring information about the art and science of measurement to framework development and the framework developers can bring information about the intentions of the frameworks to item development. As proposed in Recommendation 3-2 (in Chapter 3), implementing a change to integrate framework development and item creation will require NAGB and NCES to work together to create a structure that allows such collaboration. To some extent, NCES and NAGB already collaborate in this way,[17] but they could refocus their work on task models, rather than individual items.

Thinking in Terms of Task Models NAEP has made headway in defining task models. This approach to item development is appealing. It offers the potential to both decrease costs and increase the quality of item development, even without use of fully automatic item generation. Item review and other aspects of the quality control process can be streamlined. New items can be pre-calibrated without the cost of pilot testing. In addition, task models could be used to build in accessibility and address other issues of fairness and equity (see, e.g., Winter et al., 2018). Finally, items generated using task models can be evaluated for their ability to assess examinee knowledge and skills, providing evidence of the quality of the task model itself. NAEP's use of automated processes of item generation could then evolve as the state of the art in automatic item generation evolves.

> **RECOMMENDATION 4-2: The National Assessment Governing Board and the National Center for Education Statistics should move toward using more structured processes for item development to both**

[16]For examples of the detailed achievement-level descriptions, see, for mathematics, https://nces.ed.gov/nationsreportcard/mathematics/achieve.aspx; for science, https://nces.ed.gov/nationsreportcard/science/achieve.aspx; and for reading, https://nces.ed.gov/nationsreportcard/reading/achieve.aspx.

[17]This collaboration is implied in the documentation about the detailed achievement level. For example, see https://nces.ed.gov/nationsreportcard/mathematics/achieve.aspx.

decrease costs and improve quality. This work should include drawing from the detailed achievement-level descriptions to specify intended inferences and claims, better integrating the work of framework development and item creation, and carrying out critical aspects of review and quality control at the level of task models rather than at the level of individual items.

CHANGING THE MIX OF ITEM TYPES

NAEP currently uses a range of item types, including selected-response, constructed-response, and scenario-based tasks, as well as others. Using different item types is well suited to certain cognitive levels and content specifications, with more complex item types used to assess more complex skills. This alignment can be seen in the 4th-grade science item map, where seven of the eight items listed as above the NAEP advanced cut scores are constructed-response items.[18]

Despite this association between item types and the cognitive level and content of the items, the relation is not exact. As is often pointed out, selected-response or simpler constructed-response items can be used to assess cognitively complex material, even though there are many examples when this is not the case.[19] It is important to consider the full range of item types that can potentially be used to assess the different cognitive and content areas specified in the frameworks, rather than focusing on particular item types in the abstract.

The choice of item types is also influenced by factors other than the cognitive and content areas to be assessed, such as testing time and development, administration, and scoring costs. Changing the mix of item types could potentially change NAEP's average costs for item creation, pilot testing, test administration, and scoring. The average costs of the three item types discussed above imply that increasing the proportion of scenario-based items increases item development costs and increasing the proportion of selected-response items decreases item development costs. There are likely to be similar relationships with respect to test administration and scoring costs.

RECOMMENDATION 4-3: The National Assessment Governing Board should commission an analysis of the value and cost of different item types when multiple item types can measure the construct of

---

[18] See https://www.nationsreportcard.gov/itemmaps/?subj=SCI&grade=4&year=2019.

[19] There is recent research showing that selected-response items for which the selections are sourced from prior students' constructed responses can produce items of comparable quality in some cases (Wang et al., 2019).

interest. A full range of potential item types should be included in this analysis. The analysis should develop a framework for considering the tradeoff between value and cost. The value considered should include both the item's contribution to a score and its signal about the relevant components of the construct. The costs considered should include item development (both item creation and pilot administration), administration time, and scoring.

In addition to its implications for the cost of item development, this recommendation also relates to the costs for test administration and scoring, which are discussed in Chapters 5–7.

5

Test Administration: Moving to a Local Model

Test administration for NAEP is expensive. Because it represents about 28.6 percent of NAEP's budget, test administration presents one of the clearest opportunities for cost savings.[1] In this chapter we discuss NCES's plans to replace the current computer-based delivery model with one that is primarily school based and includes the use of local equipment and internet providers as well as school-based proctoring of the assessment. This approach could produce substantial cost savings, though with potential concerns related to standardization, comparability, equal access, and increased burden for schools. In addition to reducing the costs of regular test administration, local administration could also be used to reduce NAEP's high costs for pilot testing (see Chapter 4).

This chapter starts with a discussion of the cost of test administration for NAEP. It then outlines the program's new vision for test administration, followed by a description of the experience with local administration during the era of voluntary state participation in NAEP (prior to the No Child Left Behind Act of 2001). The fourth section addresses the challenges of local administration with computer-based delivery and the flexibility the approach offers. The fifth section considers the way the new local administration model should be reflected in the analysis of NAEP results. The final section discusses the potential for cost savings from local administration.

[1]Using the figures from Table 2-2 (in Chapter 2), $50.2 million is the average annual cost for the data collection and service and support contracts, which is 28.6 percent of NAEP's current $175.2 million total cost.

The next chapter discusses other ways of reducing test administration costs.

CURRENT COSTS

Test administration is supported by two contracts in the NAEP Alliance, one for sampling and data collection and the other for the support and service center.[2] The estimated annual average cost for these contracts is $44.8 million and $5.3 million, respectively. These average yearly costs fall much more heavily in years when the mandated reading and mathematics assessments are carried out, which require the larger samples that support state and urban district results.

The current NAEP assessment model involves sending NAEP-supported staff and devices into sampled schools. The typical cost is roughly $3,500 to $4,500 per sampled school, including the field staff that visit schools, the infrastructure to support that staff, and the devices that are brought to the schools.[3] This field work represents an average annual cost of about $36 million for an average yearly sample of 9,000 schools (see discussion in Chapter 2).

In addition, roughly 23 percent of the $21.9 million average annual cost for pilot testing is supported by the sampling and data collection contract for administration of the pilot test, representing another $5.0 million in administration costs each year.[4]

VISION FOR A DEVICE-AGNOSTIC, CONTACTLESS NAEP

The current administration model for NAEP, which uses professionally trained NAEP staff and contractors to administer the assessment, minimizes the participation burden for local schools and helps ensure quality,

[2]NCES response to Q33: The sampling and data collection contract covers the following activities: "Selects samples; prepares sampling weights; administers assessments and collects data for pilot and field tests, operational assessments, and special studies; and ships completed assessment materials to the scoring sites. Conducts the High School Transcript Study and the Middle School Transcript Study." NCES response to Q60: Of these activities, sampling accounts for 3 percent of the contract, weighting accounts for 3 percent, assessment field work accounts for 67 percent, transcript studies account for 7 percent, and infrastructure and assessment-related central office activities account for 20 percent. NCES response to Q33: The support and service center contract covers the following activities: "Provides support, training, and resources to state and TUDA [Trial Urban District Assessment] coordinators to ensure the accurate and timely sampling, administration and reporting of NAEP in each state and TUDA district."

[3]NCES response to Q70g.

[4]NCES answers to follow-up questions about evidence-centered design task models and item development costs (personal communication, June 24, 2021).

accuracy, and comparability in administration. When NAEP recently moved to computer-based delivery, the use of NCES-provided equipment was intended to reduce the burden on schools while maintaining the level of standardization that is deemed essential for NAEP. It also helped ensure that the assessment could be given in all schools, even those with limited bandwidth and technology resources.

As school staff have recently assumed increasing responsibility for state-sponsored large-scale, high-stakes assessments, which are often administered online using local devices, the current NAEP test administration model seems increasingly outdated and unnecessary. In response to these changes, and in recognition of the large costs associated with NAEP's current approach to test administration, NCES has outlined a plan to use local staff and devices for administering NAEP. NCES refers to this change as a transition to "contactless administration" because NAEP staff would no longer be directly in charge, turning it over to trained school-based staff.[5] NCES is also considering an intermediate "reduced contact" model in which NAEP staff would support test administration either virtually or with fewer in-person staff. NCES recognizes that it may have to provide equipment and proctors to some schools for a number of years and that the exact timing that will be feasible for all schools for this transition is uncertain.

LOCAL ADMINISTRATION IN THE PAPER-BASED ERA

Although NCES's plans for local test administration represent a change from NAEP's current approach, the program had extensive experience with local administration during the 1990s.[6] Prior to 2002, local education employees proctored NAEP assessments in the trial state assessment portion of the program.

The creation of the trial state assessment in 1990 led to a potentially 15-fold increase in samples, which made the professional administration model untenable given NAEP budgets at the time. However, since participation in the trial was voluntary, states that wanted to participate were asked to contribute in-kind support by supplying staff who could administer the assessment, as well as participate in the necessary training and preparation. Contractor proctors observed and audited 10 percent of the sessions.

The trial state model was used only for subjects and grades for which state results were being reported. Professional proctors continued to conduct

[5]The terms "contactless" and "reduced contact" have acquired other meanings during the COVID-19 pandemic than previous ones. This report follows the convention of "local administration" of NAEP to mean the use of local devices and local school officials as proctors.

[6]Descriptions of the operation of the state assessment during these years is based on the experience of panel member Stephen Lazer, who helped lead the work of the Educational Testing Service on NAEP during this period.

all administration in non-state subjects and grades and in private schools. Additionally, the trial state model covered only the trial administrations in a given subject and at a given grade. Since states could choose not to participate in the program, the national results were insulated from non-participation effects by keeping national and state samples strictly separate. In all but the smallest states (where the small number of students precluded two separate samples), there were separate national and state administrations in the same subject at the same grade. Since national samples did not contribute to state results and needed to maintain or allow trend comparisons to years that did not include the trial results, NAEP used professional proctoring for all schools in the national sample.

Technically, the mixed system of the 1990s worked well. However, analysts found a small difference between state and national administration models that persisted throughout the period: in matched samples, performance under the trial state model was slightly higher than in the national model. This difference necessitated an equating step to bring the results of the trial state assessment onto the national scale.

Politically, program officials viewed the "contribution in kind" as acceptable since the program was wholly voluntary. States signed up if they wanted NAEP data. If they did not wish to supply the administrators, they could forego participation in NAEP's state-level sample.

In 2001, No Child Left Behind changed the situation, with the state NAEP becoming mandatory in reading and mathematics at grades 4 and 8. To avoid having NAEP participation become an unfunded mandate, program officials asked Congress to allocate funds to allow NAEP to expand the national administration model to all schools. Since states could no longer opt out, there was also no longer a need for a separate national sample in reading and mathematics at grades 4 and 8.

CHALLENGES AND FLEXIBILITY WITH LOCAL ADMINISTRATION WITH COMPUTER-BASED DELIVERY

The planned return to local administration in a computer-based era will require local staff to address a set of issues that were absent during the trial state assessment in the 1990s. The process of preparing for assessment administration will require local staff to ensure that appropriate computer equipment and internet connections are available, in addition to helping prepare the student sample, proctoring the assessment administration, and participating in the necessary training. However, computerization over the past two decades has substantially reduced the work that local staff performed in the 1990s to prepare the student sample, read instructions for the assessment, and distribute and collect the assessment books and other assessment materials.

Since the 1990s, NAEP has also moved to include students with disabilities and English learners in its assessments.[7] Many of the accommodations to increase inclusiveness for NAEP can be implemented as universal design elements in computer-based assessments, such as providing adjustments for font size or having directions given aloud.[8] However, some accommodations, such as providing assessments in Braille or giving instructions in sign language, would require additional support from local and NAEP staff.

NAEP conducted a proof-of-concept study on the use of school-based equipment in 57 Virginia schools;[9] it uncovered several problems:

- Communication: staff who were planning administrations had incomplete information about available equipment, network and security configurations, needed setups, and available space.
- Hardware: in some schools, the hardware had low working memory and processing speed, insufficient battery charges, cracked screens, or missing keys.
- Connectivity problems: in some cases, poor connection speeds, lagging and freezing, and access to bandwidth competed with other school demands.
- Technical support: access to technical support was uneven across the studied schools, with some schools needing unavailable help troubleshooting problems and monitoring administration progress.

These difficulties are similar to those seen in other programs that have used or tried to use local equipment to administer large-scale standardized exams (see, e.g., Brown, 2019; Herold, 2016; Strauss, 2020).

At this time, familiarity with the computer technology and its use in assessment continues to advance, particularly with the now-widespread use of computer-based administration for state assessments. The remote arrangements that many schools and districts were able to make during the pandemic to carry out assessment virtually from students' homes illustrate how far the technology has come, though many barriers remain, and inequities persist (Michel, 2021). In light of the barriers and inequities that were highlighted by experiences during the pandemic, many districts used

---

[7]See https://nces.ed.gov/nationsreportcard/about/inclusion.asp.

[8]See https://nces.ed.gov/nationsreportcard/about/accom_table.aspx.

[9]The Virginia proof-of-concept study is described in a PowerPoint presentation by A. Deigan, Exploring eNAEP's Design. Presented to the NAEP Validity Studies Panel, National Center for Education Statistics, 2021, Feb. 11. The presentation was provided to the panel and is available in the project's Public Access File. Note that the proof-of-concept study was carried out in a state that has a history of successfully administering its state test online. Other states without such experience may experience greater problems than did Virginia in the local administration of NAEP.

funding from the American Rescue Plan to make further improvements to their technology infrastructure (AASA, 2021).

NCES's plans for local administration call for school-based staff to conduct readiness checks for available equipment before each administration. NCES will need to create a scalable and efficient process to validate that schools are using equipment that conforms to NAEP requirements. School equipment will need to accommodate NAEP's innovative item types[10] and ensure that test questions and answer options display correctly and load quickly in a consistent manner from student to student and from school to school across the country. These requirements would certainly include detailed specifications for laptop computers and tablets.[11] Examples of minimum requirements might cover screen size and resolution, touch screen capabilities, mouse and track pad/ball capabilities, keyboard size and general layout (e.g., not allowing virtual keyboards or enhanced gaming keyboards), memory and processing capabilities, acceptable operating system versions, internet browsers or cloud applications, and bandwidth.[12]

Furthermore, with a local model, school-based staff will need to provide technical assistance for hardware-related issues, with a school technology coordinator who can serve as the first level of technical support when issues arise during the testing period. Off-site NAEP staff will be needed to address questions that may be out of the scope of school technology coordinators.

The local staff who provide technical support for the equipment and address the software issues will need training. So will the staff who administer the assessments. While traditional models for training have been in person (Hoagwood et al., 2018), the COVID-19 pandemic has accelerated a shift to online training, with improvements in its quality and effectiveness (Lockee, 2021). The use of online training will result in cost saving and simplification compared to the 1990s experience of local administration.

Results from the Virginia proof-of-concept study (Deigan, 2021) indicate that school contexts and access to the necessary equipment differ markedly. NAEP's local administration plans assume that the model will not be feasible in some places because of limited equipment or other barriers. Since NAEP selects a representative sample of schools to reflect the demographics of the nation, it is important that a high proportion of selected schools and students participate. In cases where the local administration model will be difficult to implement, it will have to be tailored to the local

[10]See Chapter 2.

[11]Given the complications of small devices, the requirement would likely exclude notepads and smartphones.

[12]There has been some discussion in the context of eNAEP (see Chapter 9) about developing dedicated cloud-based NAEP test delivery applications to bypass some of the display and interactive limitations of internet browser–based applications.

context, with NAEP-supported equipment and staff provided as needed. The NAEP program may find it efficient to institute a routine process for approving certain schools to automatically receive additional equipment and possibly staff to support the administration. This might include, for example, schools that qualify for free or reduced-price lunch or have large percentages of students who qualify, or schools in rural or remote areas, or other criteria. Augmentation to the NAEP state coordinator program may also be needed to find appropriate ways to support schools.

The additional activities that school staff will need to carry out may also suggest a role for some stipend or other financial support for local administration of NAEP, particularly for schools that are not yet routinely administering their state assessments digitally. Such financial support would help avoid the impression that a shift to local administration is an exercise in cost-shifting from the NAEP program to local schools. At the same time, however, providing substantial support to every participating school could eliminate any net savings from a change to local administration. In addition, the burden for local school staff is likely to decrease over time—with increases in computing power and staff familiarity with digitally based assessment—but it could be politically difficult to end a policy of financial support once established unless it is clearly framed as transitional.

In addition to the challenges described above, the new approach could also potentially provide some flexibility that could help schools in administering NAEP. The current administration approach is designed to minimize costs to the program by using the NAEP-supported proctors and equipment as efficiently as possible. As a result, the current model simultaneously assesses as many sampled students as possible in a school. However, with a local administration model, schools could administer assessments to sampled students over a multiweek window, which would allow a large number of students to be tested on a small number of machines available in a library or media center. This small-group approach to administering would require a somewhat different approach for local proctoring and program auditing. Although this approach would not appreciably affect NAEP program costs, the flexibility could substantially simplify the difficulties some schools may have in administering NAEP by avoiding the need to provide large rooms equipped with many computers that meet NAEP's requirements.

RECOMMENDATION 5-1: The National Center for Education Statistics (NCES) should continue to develop its plan to administer NAEP using local school staff as proctors with online assessment delivery on local school computers, with development and bridge studies as needed to understand the feasibility and effects of this change in different contexts. This new model should be accompanied by adequate training and support of school staff, including tailored support for schools with

more limited resources that may need NCES to provide proctors and equipment. NCES should also explore the use of flexible administration windows to allow schools to develop plans that accommodate local constraints on available equipment and consider appropriate ways to compensate local schools for their contributions to the administration, especially during the transition to this new model.

RETHINKING STANDARDIZATION WITH LOCAL ADMINISTRATION

NAEP has traditionally taken a strong view regarding standardization by providing both the test materials and proctors to each testing site, and, currently, also the software, computers, and network equipment for administering the assessments digitally. In addition to the expense involved, high levels of standardization may actually have adverse consequences regarding NAEP's generalizability and utility in the presence of ubiquitous and ongoing technological changes in teaching, learning, and assessment.

Standardization in testing implies that as many of the important *conditions of measurement* are held constant as practicable. Those conditions are usually introduced as constraints that include administering a fixed-length test form comprised of the same or highly similar test items to all examinees using the same mode of delivery, as well as following a consistent set of item formats, time limits, and test administration instructions (American Educational Research Association, American Psychological Association, and National Council on Measurement in Education, 2014). The two chief motivations for standardization are *fairness*—operationalized as applying consistent conditions of measurement for everyone—and the need for *score comparability* over time.[13] However, conditions of measurement will undoubtedly change as the constructs evolve and assessment technologies change.

There is also no guarantee that strong standardization that penalizes examinees who are unfamiliar with one or more of the conditions of measurement is actually fairer than universally customizing the testing experience to equally facilitate all examinees. Testing students on familiar technology may allow them to put forth their best performance.[14] For example, the provision of a word processing application developed exclusively for NAEP testing cannot guarantee fairness and comparability when the

---

[13]Score comparability across conditions only holds if test takers are assigned under all conditions or at least randomly assigned to various conditions of measurement. Holding them constant does not allow comparisons across conditions.

[14]Note that this point is closely related to the arguments made in support of providing accommodations in assessment.

features, functionality, and interface may differ from what (some) examinees use in their everyday learning activities. Way and Strain-Seymour (2021) summarize the research related to 17 different device-related factors that may affect student performance on NAEP.

As noted above, the move to local test administration assumes that NAEP will develop some minimum specifications for devices, operating systems, network configurations, and connectivity that can be used to administer the assessments. These specifications will allow the assessment to be administered in a relatively common way, while falling short of the complete standardization that NAEP currently enforces by providing its own equipment. There will inevitability still be substantial variability across classes of equipment, operation systems, and network configurations that meet NAEP's minimum requirements for local test administration. This variability reflects both the practical reality of using local devices and the necessary customization to allow students to use devices that are familiar to them.

To allow NAEP to account for the effects of equipment variability in the analysis of assessment results, the program will need to collect detailed information from the testing sites about the equipment and the operating systems used. This can be done as part of the readiness checks that are performed to ensure that the equipment meets the minimum requirements. The device characteristics can then be used to develop categorical classes of equipment and systems to use during analysis of the assessment results (Luecht, 2005, 2006, 2016). Such analyses would include using item response theory to evaluate item and person data-model misfit and carrying out residual analysis. Influential differences in different classes of equipment could then be incorporated into the assessment modeling and calibration framework, though it would be important to consider the potential effect of any correlations between classes of equipment and student characteristics and contexts. Modeling the variation across equipment classes as random effects would allow the resulting estimates to reflect generalization across devices, which is the construct of interest for NAEP since the frameworks are not focused on device-specific competencies. Furthermore, the program can use the results related to different equipment classes to update the program's equipment requirements over time and to calibrate results across years as the mix of devices changes.

RECOMMENDATION 5-2: Since a key component of moving to local administration will be the development of minimum requirements for equipment, operating systems, and connectivity, information about local devices and administration conditions will have to be included in the data collection. Analysts should use statistical techniques that account for the effects of differences in devices and other local conditions

to produce estimates that generalize across those differences. The National Center for Education Statistics should explore the use of random effects and other statistical techniques to produce estimates that reflect generalization across devices.

ANTICIPATED COST SAVINGS FROM LOCAL ADMINISTRATION

NCES estimates that development costs for the transition to an online, device-agnostic, contactless model will total $18 million. These development costs involve a series of proofs of concept and field test studies to examine the use of two hardware options—NAEP-provided non-touch screen Chromebooks and school equipment—with reduced field staff. The estimated development costs also support the cost of a bridge study in 2024 to look at the transition between NAEP-provided touch screen Surface Pros and NAEP-provided non–touch screen Chromebooks.[15]

Initially, NCES expected the new model to save $52 million from 2026 through 2030 for the mandated assessments in reading and mathematics in grades 4 and 8, though that projection has evolved as the development work continues.[16] In the latest estimates, as this report was being prepared, NCES projects that the proportion of schools using local administration will grow from 40 percent in 2026 to 67 percent in 2028 and to 80 percent in 2030.[17] This growth in the projected proportion of schools using local administration is accompanied by a reduction of per-school administration costs of roughly 20 percent in 2026, 32.5 percent in 2028, and 37.5 percent in 2030, in comparison with the current baseline.[18]

The NCES estimates were based on an initial sample of 15,500 schools for the mandated assessments, which would produce an administration cost of roughly $62 million in the baseline year of 2024.[19] The reductions in administration costs would imply total reductions compared to the baseline starting with $12.4 million in 2026, and then $20.2 million in 2028, and $23.3 million in 2030. These projected savings total about $56 million from local administration.

---

[15]NCES response to Q57c. NCES does not expect to require bridge studies to move from NAEP-provided non–touch screen Chromebooks to school equipment or to move to reduce contact or contactless administration.

[16]NCES response to Q57d and cost driver PowerPoint provided by NCES (personal communication, May 13, 2021).

[17]NCES response to Q70a.

[18]Cost-per-school figures from NCES (personal communication, November 10, 2021). The current estimated costs per school for administration are $2,700 to $3,700 in 2026, $2,200 to $3,200 in 2028, and $2,000 to $3,000 in 2030. We used the midpoint for each year in calculating the projected reductions.

[19]Cost-per-school figures from NCES (personal communication, November 10, 2021).

It is not clear to the panel why local administration is projected to reduce costs by less than half for the schools in which it is used. The panel did not have access to a breakdown between the different types of costs related to the field teams—combining the field staff, infrastructure, and devices that support the schools. However, a local administration model would be expected to substantially reduce all of these major costs, and we do not understand what major new costs could arise that would be half again as large.

NCES notes that training costs could be higher with local administration.[20] This is possible, but it seems that this extra cost should be modest, given the likelihood that remote instruction can be used for training.

NCES also notes that auditing would be done in some schools, but that would clearly involve a small portion of the schools and perhaps only a single NAEP staff member rather than a team of several people.[21] NCES also notes that increased help-desk support would be required, but again the level of cost required for such support would be expected to be substantially lower than sending teams to each school to administer the assessments.[22] Even if NAEP continued to have some staff onsite or available electronically rather than unassisted local administration, fewer NAEP staff members would be used for each school, and there would still be expected savings related to devices.

NCES does not currently expect to provide payments to schools for local administration as reimbursements for costs or incentives for participation.[23] Given the increasing familiarity with administering assessments online that is likely over the coming decade, the panel agrees with this position over the long term; however, as noted above, it might be reasonable to consider some stipend for schools during the initial transition to local administration when the approach is relatively new.

After schools gain experience with local administration, the panel expects substantially larger savings are possible than are suggested by current NCES estimates, especially when considering increased familiarity by 2030 with computers in general and computer assessment in particular across the entire education system. In addition, the panel expects that it would be reasonable to extend the local administration model to the full set of assessments, substantially reducing the average annual administration costs of $36 million and the average annual pilot administration costs of $5.0 million.

---

[20]NCES response to Q57d.

[21]NCES response to Q70c; the response suggests that perhaps 10 to 15 percent of schools with contactless administration would be audited.

[22]NCES response to Q57d.

[23]NCES response to Q57d.

As an initial approximation, the panel estimates that the program can reasonably aim for a percentage reduction in administration costs that is much closer to the percentage of schools using the local administration model. This would suggest an expected annual savings closer to 80 percent of the current administration costs if NCES expects that 80 percent of the schools can use local administration. This estimate in turn suggests an estimated annual savings of roughly $28.8 million for assessment administration and $4.0 million for pilot testing by 2030. The total estimated savings of $32.8 million represents 18.7 percent of the current NAEP budget.

NCES notes[24] that the adaptations for assessment administration post-COVID-19 may suggest substantial increases in administration costs that are not yet understood. It is important to note that a widespread use of local administration is likely to reverse these extra cost increases, since special procedures for going into the schools will not be necessary if NAEP staff do not go into the schools. As a result, there may be large new administration costs in the next few years that would be mirrored by equivalent large decreases in administration as the transition to local administration proceeds.

RECOMMENDATION 5-3: The National Center for Education Statistics (NCES) should review its estimates of the potential cost savings from local administration of the mandated assessments in reading and mathematics in grades 4 and 8. The estimated savings are unexpectedly small when local administration would largely eliminate the large current costs for traveling proctors and equipment, even after considering any offsetting additional costs for training and technological infrastructure. NCES should also consider the use of the local administration model for reducing costs of all other assessments, as well as the costs for the pilot administration of new items.

[24]Information from NCES (personal communication, November 10, 2021).

6

Test Administration: Other Possible Innovations

Chapter 5 discussed the efficiencies and cost savings in test administration associated with the transition to a locally based model and Chapter 4 discussed the consideration of the mix of item types, which could indirectly affect administration time. This chapter discusses four other possible strategies that could also be explored to reduce the cost of test administration: increasing the information gathered from each sampled student by testing them for longer periods to include two subjects; conducting statistical power analyses to reevaluate the sample sizes needed to support the desired comparisons; increasing the efficiency of testing time by using computer-adaptive testing methods; and sharing administration resources with NCES's international assessments for assessments with overlapping student populations.[1]

In all cases, the potential savings from the innovations discussed in this chapter would be dampened by a move to the local administration model (detailed in Chapter 5). That is, the innovations discussed in this chapter potentially provide other ways to reduce administration costs, but a successful transition to local test administration would substantially reduce field costs, which would substantially reduce the possibility for these innovations to save money. However, several of the innovations offer the

[1]Another set of strategies using artificial intelligence could provide opportunities to support the proctoring of tests during administration by such means as monitoring test-taker behavior with computer vision and real-time analysis of process data; however, the panel concluded that they would be too controversial for a mandated federal program related to K–12 education.

possibility of reducing the burden on schools or students, which is also an important objective.

TESTING TWO UNRELATED SUBJECTS FOR EACH STUDENT

NCES is currently exploring the possibility of assessing two unrelated subjects by testing students for a longer time, with 90 rather than 60 minutes for the cognitive items. Originally, this plan was designed to allow three 30-minute blocks of cognitive items rather than two, with two blocks for one subject and one block for the other.[2] More recently, NCES is looking at a model using a short router (see "Adaptive Testing," below) and one longer block for each subject, totaling 90 minutes.[3] Other models are possible, including using the extra block of time to pilot new items, which is one approach that could be used to reduce NAEP's high costs for pilot testing (see Chapter 4).

NCES estimates that two-subject administration would require an investment of $10 million to cover three studies, two in 2026 to examine a two-subject design, one with a traditional linear test design and one with adaptive test design, and a bridge study in 2028.[4]

NCES estimates that two-subject administration would allow sample sizes to be reduced by one-third without changing NAEP's precision.[5] The estimates include an expectation that multisubject testing will be coupled with adaptive testing, but the sample size reduction would largely be based on the extra time per student.[6] NCES estimates that two-subject NAEP testing will save $17 million from 2028 through 2030.

As discussed in Chapter 5, NCES currently estimates the savings from the use of local administration for the mandated assessments by a cost reduction from $3,500–4,500 per school in 2024 to $2,000–3,000 in 2030 over a base of 15,500 schools. The expected savings from two-subject administration produces further savings by reducing the number of sampled schools by one-third, initially to 13,500 in 2028 and then to 10,500 in 2030.[7] In 2028 there would be 2,000 fewer schools when the per-school

---

[2]Interestingly, NAEP did try a three-block, two-subject design in the 1985–1986 administration (Beaton et al., 1988).

[3]NCES (personal communication, December 17, 2021).

[4]NCES response to Q57e.

[5]NCES response to Q57f.

[6]NCES response to Q71a. Although "an adaptive design likely will not result in significant sample size reductions or error reductions to the two-subject design," in the context of two-subject designs, "adaptive design could potentially help to stabilize the group score estimation when, as an outcome of the two-subject design, the testing time for half of the student sample on a given subject is less than what's currently offered in NAEP."

[7]Cost-per-school figures from NCES (personal communication, November 10, 2021).

cost is expected to be $2,700, and in 2030 there would be 5,000 fewer schools when the per-school cost is expected to be $2,500.[8] These estimates produce a savings of $17.9 million for the 2 years.

The use of tests with 90 minutes for the cognitive items across all NAEP assessments has the potential to reduce the number of sampled schools and overall administration costs by roughly one-third. If the panel's estimate is correct that local administration has the potential to reduce administration costs by about 80 percent, then the remaining average annual administration costs in a decade should be roughly 20 percent of their current values: $7.2 million for the assessments and $1.0 million for the pilot administration.[9] If 90-minute tests can reduce these administration costs by one-third, that might represent an annual average savings of $2.7 million by 2030, which is 1.6 percent of NAEP's overall budget.

The potential savings in the next few years from using tests with 90 minutes for the cognitive items—before local administration is implemented—would be much larger because the overall administration costs are currently much larger. For example, a one-third reduction of the current average annual assessment administration cost of $36 million would be $12 million.

In addition to the potential cost savings for administration, joint information about student performance on two subjects could provide additional information about the dependencies in proficiency across subjects by looking at the relationships between the subjects by student.[10]

There are several issues that need to be addressed to decide if multi-subject testing is feasible for NAEP. In particular, the program needs to investigate the effects of longer testing time in relation to its impact on both student results and on the scheduling for schools. Although either of these factors could pose problems, many state assessments are longer than NAEP's typical two-block assessments and, as noted in Chapter 2, NAEP has already tried longer assessments in science and technology and engineering literacy.

Beyond the longer testing time, there are issues related to balancing subject order across blocks, estimating plausible values[11] from one-subject

[8]Cost-per-school figures from NCES (personal communication, November 10, 2021). Midpoints used for each range given for the cost per school.

[9]See Chapter 5 for the calculation of an average annual assessment administration cost of $36 million and an average annual pilot administration cost of $2.5 million; the figures in the above test use 20 percent of these two figures.

[10]Joint performance information might also provide information related to the potential integration of two subjects; see discussion in Chapter 3.

[11]See the discussion of plausible values in "Structure" in Chapter 2.

blocks, and designing an appropriate bridging study for the transition.[12] NCES is aware of the challenges related to moving to longer dual-subject tests and has designed a study to evaluate the impact of these changes well ahead of any adoptions. The study was originally scheduled for 2021 and was delayed by the pandemic.

RECOMMENDATION 6-1: The National Center for Education Statistics (NCES) should continue to develop its plan to administer NAEP in longer sessions that allow for 90 minutes for the testing of cognitive items for each student. NCES should explore other models for using longer tests, in addition to its current plan. The decision to use longer tests should be based primarily on their potential to reduce testing burden by reducing the number of sampled students and to understand dependencies in proficiency across subjects, rather than being based on any long-term cost savings, which would be minimal with local test administration.

RECONSIDERING THE SAMPLE SIZES NEEDED TO ACHIEVE NAEP'S PURPOSES

Test administration costs—particularly in the current model—are directly related to the size of NAEP's sample. If it is possible for NAEP to perform its mission with smaller sample sizes, there could be substantial cost reductions.

Assessing NAEP's statistical power and its corresponding costs requires specifying the target parameters for estimation. Although technical considerations can inform the choice of target parameters, the desired parameters here are ultimately a policy determination. The implied questions that NAEP answers are referenced in the NAGB statement of NAEP's purpose:[13]

> NAEP results describe educational achievement for groups of students at a single point in time, progress in educational achievement for groups of students over time, and differential educational achievement and progress among jurisdictions and subpopulations.

This statement implies several target parameters. At the highest level, there is achievement at a single point in time, for example, an average scaled score for a single state or the country. In addition, there is progress over

[12] "Plans for Design of 2021 NAEP Reading and Mathematics Assessments," PowerPoint presentation by Enis Dogan and Helena Jia to the NAGB Meeting, March 6, 2020. Available in the project Public Access File.

[13] See https://www.nagb.gov/content/dam/nagb/en/documents/what-we-do/quarterly-board-meeting-materials/2020-03/11-intended-meaning-of-naep.pdf, p. 2.

time, for example, the change in mean achievement scores in a state or the country from 2017 to 2019. NAGB's statement also specifies "differential progress among jurisdictions," which amounts to asking whether one state or urban district makes more educational progress than another. Because this last question compares two mean differences, this is a "difference in differences." Then, the statement mentions differential progress "among jurisdictions and subpopulations." This parameter amounts to asking, for example, whether gender gaps are increasing more in one state than another. Because this compares a gap over time, in two different states, this is sometimes called a "triple difference."

As an example, consider the 2019 NAEP estimate for the performance of English-language learners in Shelby County, Tennessee, which is one of the urban districts included in the Trial Urban District Assessment program. The mean score of this population was estimated to be 180, with a standard error of 4.1.[14] Assuming the same standard error in 2 years, a trend difference would need to be 11.4 points (an effect size of roughly .33) to be statistically significant at the 5 percent level. And if one wanted to compare that trend difference in Shelby County to the trend difference in another jurisdiction (with comparable standard error), the difference in trends for English-language learners between the two jurisdictions would have to be 16.1 points to be statistically significant.

With a larger sample, NAEP's estimates would be more precise. For example, if the sample for Shelby County doubled in size, the standard error would decrease roughly to 2.9 and it would be possible to detect a trend difference for Shelby County as small as 8.1 points.[15] Conversely, if the sample for Shelby County were cut in half, the standard error would increase to 5.8, and the smallest trend difference that could be detected for Shelby County alone would be 16.1 points.

There is a direct relationship between the size of NAEP's sample and the performance differences that NAEP can detect. The size of the score-level differences that are educationally and politically meaningful for comparing student performance across jurisdictions over time and across groups can be used to determine the sample size needed for NAEP to be able to detect those differences, which will then affect the cost of NAEP's data collections.

An analysis of NAEP's statistical power could determine if NAEP can identify the performance differences that are educationally and politically

[14]NAEP results can be obtained from the NAEP Data Explorer at https://nces.ed.gov/nationsreportcard/data. The "generate reports" link can be used to specify "global formatting options," which can include providing standard errors.

[15]We note that the simple numerical comparisons in this paragraph ignore the complexities of calculating standard errors in NAEP, which require (among other things) considerations of student clustering within schools, the sparsity of observations for each student, and the number of test items given to each student.

meaningful even with a substantially smaller sample than is collected today. However, it is possible that such an analysis could instead suggest that NAEP actually requires larger samples to detect the kinds of performance differences that are educationally and politically meaningful.[16]

RECOMMENDATION 6-2: The National Center for Education Statistics should commission an analysis of the tradeoff between NAEP's sample sizes and its statistical power in detecting differences in performance, including trends and gaps, and its ability to achieve minimum cell sizes for reporting on subpopulations. In particular, this analysis should consider the stated purposes of the National Assessment Governing Board to measure not only average scores, but also differences over time and between targeted subpopulations, and it should provide evidence about the level of precision required for these results to be meaningful to educators and policy makers. Evidence about meaningful levels of statistical power and minimum cell sizes for subpopulations should be directly related to the implications for NAEP's sample sizes and associated administration costs.

ADAPTIVE TESTING

Computerized adaptive testing has been effectively used in large-scale testing since the mid-1990s. A typical adaptive test sequentially administers test questions and uses students' responses to assign subsequent questions at appropriate levels of difficulty until scores reach prescribed levels of precision or decision accuracy. Computer-adaptive multistage testing is a variation in which the adaptation occurs for groups of items, rather than for individual items (Luecht, 2014). A well-documented advantage of adaptive testing is that it can efficiently improve the accuracy of individual and aggregated scores or reduce test time while maintaining accuracy (Lord, 1980; Ul Hassan and Miller, 2019; van der Linden and Pashley, 2010; Verschoor et al., 2019).

In principle, the optimization offered by adaptive testing could be used to decrease the size of NAEP's sample, reducing administration costs and the burden on schools and students. The potential route for such cost savings relates to the two innovations discussed above: longer testing of two unrelated subjects and improving estimates at low proficiency levels.

Saving Costs with Adaptive Testing through Longer Testing of Two Unrelated Subjects Because adaptive testing is more efficient than traditional

[16]Mosquin and Chromy (2004) discuss the NAEP sample sizes needed for detecting policy-meaningful improvements in states in the context of the No Child Left Behind Act.

testing, it can result in shorter tests: successively selecting test questions likely to yield the most information about a student's proficiency means students need to answer fewer questions to obtain an accurate estimate, allowing a shorter test. If total testing time turns out to be a key barrier to testing two unrelated subjects, adaptive testing could help reduce testing time to make the approach feasible. However, as described below, such reductions are likely to be modest, given the nature of NAEP's items. Additionally, there may be simpler ways to cut back on time if that turns out to be necessary for testing two unrelated subjects without the challenges associated with adaptive testing: blocks could simply be reduced from 30 to 25 minutes, which was their length for many years.

Saving Costs with Adaptive Testing through Improving Estimates at Low Proficiency Levels Adaptive testing can be used to improve the precision of individual scores, particularly at the high and low ends of the ability distribution, without incurring the additional cost for larger samples that might otherwise be required. Although NAEP does not report individual scores, adaptive testing has the potential to increase the precision of group estimates at the ends of the ability distribution and for jurisdictions with relatively small sample sizes. For the most part, NAEP obtains defensible and accurate estimates of the performance of lower-performing populations, but estimates for these populations tend to have higher standard errors than similarly sized populations at the middle and higher ends of the NAEP scales. Recent policy interest in NAEP has tended to focus on groups whose scores are often imprecisely estimated (Oranje et al., 2014, p. 378). For example, urban districts that are now estimated in the Trial Urban District Assessment program have smaller samples than states and tend to perform on average at lower levels on the scale; both differences result in higher standard errors. If NAEP starts to target its statistical precision more closely to a specific level necessary for policy decisions, with a goal to reduce sample sizes, adaptive testing could help ensure that statistical precision is adequate for lower-performing populations.

In addition to these cost-related reasons for considering adaptive testing, there are other potential benefits of the approach. Adaptive tests can improve the test-taking experiences of students at the low end by focusing more of the items at a test taker's level. An improved test experience is important for a voluntary testing program for which there are no external motivations for doing well.

Although there are potential cost and non-cost benefits from adaptive testing, there would be significant challenges to implementing it for NAEP. The biggest barrier to the use of adaptive testing comes from several characteristics of the NAEP assessment frameworks:

- Multi-item sets: Some subjects use a single stimulus for a large number of items.[17] Because the items in these item sets typically vary in difficulty and the item sets themselves are not differentially difficult, these long sets of items do not allow significant adaptive routing within blocks (Swain et al., 2018).
- Items requiring human scoring: All NAEP frameworks make extensive use of constructed-response items, many of which currently require human scoring (but see discussion in Chapter 8). This requirement limits any routing decisions to only the portion of the construct that is reflected by the machine-scorable items.
- Subscale reporting: Some subjects call for subscale reporting, including both reading and mathematics. Subscales limit the efficiency of any adaptive approach because the adaptation needs to reflect each of the different subscales.

In addition to problems related to the frameworks, there are some costs related to a transition to adaptive testing. They include the investments needed to develop larger item pools for the low and high ends of the ability distribution that tend to be poorly covered in traditional tests, the costs of reassembling existing items into blocks at different levels of difficulty, and the cost of developing the technology for adaptive testing. These added costs would be justified by the opportunity to provide better information across the full range of student abilities, but they limit the ability to use adaptive testing to reduce costs.

Because of the requirements of NAEP's frameworks, computer-adaptive testing at the item level and across all subscales is not practical. The practical problems can be addressed in multistage adaptive testing, in which the adaptation occurs over groups of items and the first stage is limited to items that can be automatically scored, but this approach may prevent the use of some item types and may omit consideration of some subscales in the adaptation. NCES has been investigating the use of multistage adaptive testing at least since 2011 (Oranje et al., 2014, p. 374). In the simplest version, the first stage used for adaptation may have the characteristics of a simple screener for routing test takers to full cognitive blocks at different levels of difficulty, an approach that NCES has recently started to consider.[18] The coarse adaptation that is possible is unlikely to result in substantial efficiencies across the full population, but it could improve estimates for some groups, particularly low-performing students. At the same time, however,

[17]The reading *Framework* (NAGB, 2019b) is the most prominent example of this approach.
[18]NCES (personal communication, December 17, 2021).

this approach could raise problems if the screener indicates the advisability of below-grade testing for which there is no framework.

RECOMMENDATION 6-3: The National Center for Education Statistics (NCES) should not pursue adaptive testing for NAEP as a way of saving costs, but the agency should continue to investigate its use for its potential to improve the precision of statistical estimates and the test-taking experiences for low-performing students. NCES should also consider that no single approach to adaptive testing may fit all subjects and that some changes to assessment frameworks may be necessary to facilitate adaptive administration.

COORDINATING RESOURCES WITH NCES'S INTERNATIONAL ASSESSMENTS

In addition to NAEP, NCES sponsors two major international assessments for which data are collected in U.S. schools, the Trends in International Mathematics and Science Study (TIMSS) and the Program for International Student Assessment. NCES also conducts linking studies to connect these assessments. Currently, all these assessments use separate instruments and independent data collections. In the mid-2010s NCES considered an effort to integrate these assessments (as the "NCES Integrated Assessment System") to coordinate data collection and promote sharing of item pools and even assessment components.[19]

In principle, the integration of sampling and data collection activities across education surveys could result in substantial cost savings, as well as improve the quality of data collected and facilitate a range of special studies and linking activities. However, realizing these improvements would require a high level of coordination across separate programs.

The easiest way to recognize efficiencies in NCES assessments would be to coordinate the data collections for the school-based assessments, while leaving the structure and content of the assessments intact. For example, in a year in which both NAEP and TIMSS were in the field, one might assign TIMSS sessions to schools that had been sampled for NAEP and then administer both assessments on the same visit. However, to reach this modest level of integration and achieve the savings it could potentially produce, it would be necessary to agree on a common assessment window, sampling schedule and plan, data collection contract, set of teacher and school questionnaires, and set of accommodations and exclusion policies. This level of

[19]NIAS Concept Paper (TR-0324), internal NCES document. Provided to the panel and available in the project's Public Access File.

coordination would be daunting to obtain across assessment programs that are each responsible to separate policy-making bodies.

Greater efficiencies and flexibilities could be realized if data collection were coordinated within assessment sessions and not solely at the school level. For example, within any classroom, some students might be taking NAEP while others were taking TIMSS, with still others receiving content from both assessments to facilitate linking. This approach would require further agreement on a common platform for technology delivery, assessment length, and block structure.

Even without reaching the level of coordinating the content of different assessments, the practical and political costs involved in achieving this level of coordination across separate assessment programs is likely to be overwhelming.

RECOMMENDATION 6-4: Efforts to coordinate NAEP test administration with the international assessment programs sponsored by the National Center for Education Statistics should not be used as a strategy to reduce costs.

7

Item Scoring

Item scoring for NAEP is expensive because of the extensive use of constructed-response and scenario-based tasks that have, to date, required human scoring. This chapter first provides an overview of NAEP's current costs for scoring and then discusses automated scoring, which is an innovation being pursued by NAEP's sponsors to reduce scoring costs for constructed-response and scenario-based tasks.

CURRENT COSTS[1]

Scoring for the state-level samples of reading and mathematics costs about $2.5 million per grade or about $8 per assessed student.[2] Thus, the cost for scoring the average annual rate of 400,000 students is about $3.2 million across all assessments, which is 1.8 percent of NAEP's budget.

Test scoring is covered by one contract in the NAEP Alliance, which is for scoring and dissemination.[3] The estimated annual average cost of this contract is $8.3 million (see Table 2-2 in Chapter 2).

[1]After a prepublication version of the report was provided to Institute of Education Sciences, NCES, and NAGB, this section was edited to clarify the description of the costs of the scoring and dissemination contract that are not related to scoring.

[2]NCES response to Q57b.

[3]NCES response to Q33. The scoring and dissemination contract, also referred to as the materials, distribution, processing, and scoring contract, includes the following activities: "Prepares and packages all assessment and auxiliary materials; distributes assessment booklets and materials to the test administrators for each school; receives the materials from the schools; with [item development] and [design, analysis and reporting] contractor develops scoring training materials; and scores all assessments."

The estimated annual average cost for the other activities in the contract is $5.1 million. As indicated in the title of the contract, it includes a set of activities related to materials, distribution, and processing.[4] It is reasonable to expect that computer-based administration (discussed in Chapters 5 and 6) will largely eliminate most of these activities in the future. The contract also includes six activities related to management and reporting[5] and one activity to support assessment administration.[6] Finally, the contract includes an optional activity for unspecified special studies. The panel does not have a breakdown between these different types of costs.

AUTOMATED SCORING OF CONSTRUCTED-RESPONSE ITEMS

Automated scoring[7] refers to the "assignment of a score to a constructed response, produced by a test taker in response to a task or prompt, by means of a computational algorithm" (Bejar, 2011, p. 319).[8] Automated scoring makes use of statistical and computational linguistic methods in order to model scores assigned by human raters. The model focuses on specific features in students' responses and uses those features to generate a score, intended to mimic the process used by human scorers. Automated scoring has been widely adopted in K–12 assessment, licensure, and certification programs and is one of the most recognized applications of machine learning in educational measurement (Foltz, Yan, and Rupp, 2020).[9]

---

[4]NCES response to Q69e. There are six contract activities listed related to materials, distribution, and processing: acquiring materials and supplies; spiral and bundle materials; distribute assessment materials to schools; track and receive assessment materials from schools; receipt control; and data capture and processing.

[5]NCES response to Q69e. The six contract activities related to management and reporting are listed as follows: administrative reports; quality control; contractor meetings; information collections requests for Office of Management and Budget approval; technical documentation web page; and NAGB attendance, preparation, and support.

[6]NCES response to Q69e. The activity to support assessment administration is described as follows: "State Service Center, State NAEP Coordinators, and State Testing Directors support."

[7]"Automated scoring" and "machine scoring" are sometimes used as equivalent terms. However, in this section, we distinguish automated scoring from machine scoring: automated scoring deals with unstructured input, such as unconstrained text, and machine scoring deals with structured input (e.g., math equations) or technology-enabled item inputs (e.g., ordered elements, drop-down boxes, and machine-enabled plots or graphs). With this distinction in mind, this section addresses automated scoring, not machine scoring, because NAEP already uses machine scoring for items that can be scored with other techniques; it is the items that allow unconstrained constructed responses that are still often routed for human scoring.

[8]The implementation of that algorithm is referred to as a scoring engine.

[9]See also *An Overview of the Use of Automated Scoring Systems in Operational Assessments,* AIR-ESSIN technical memorandum for task 14, 2020. Internal document provided to the panel by NCES and available in the project's Public Access File.

Automated-scoring models have displayed comparable performance relative to humans[10] when scoring short and long essays and constructed responses in reading comprehension and mathematics (Cahill et al., 2020; McGraw-Hill Education CTB, 2014; Partnership for Assessment of Readiness for College and Careers, 2015; Shermis and Hamner, 2013),[11] though there is some evidence that the comparability between human and machine scoring is weaker for some groups, such as English-language learners.[12] Automated scoring has also been successfully applied to mathematical expressions and equations entered using an equation editor or to graphing items using a graph interface (Fife, 2017).

NAEP has conducted studies to evaluate the feasibility of automated scoring of assessments of writing, reading, history, and civics.[13] These studies found that currently available scoring engines can successfully mimic human scoring in writing—but not yet in the other subjects—using standards widely accepted within the field (Williamson, Xi, and Breyer, 2012).

The incorporation of automated scoring into NAEP offers a number of likely benefits, including faster scoring, improved score consistency within and across administrations, higher-quality scoring of items when combined with human scoring, increased information about student responses, and potentially cost savings. Importantly, automated-scoring models do not drift and can help ensure that the scoring rubrics are applied consistently across years to support the estimates of trend. However, automated scoring models require human monitoring to examine performance, and models may need recalibration. Automated scoring also offers the potential for collecting additional diagnostic information about student responses beyond a score. Spelling, coherence, syntactic variation, and other linguistic features collected during the scoring process can provide more insights about student knowledge and skills. This is especially significant for a program that provides data that can support population-level inferences.

Many NAEP items in mathematics, reading, and writing may be machine scorable with available technologies. Importantly, the rapid improvements in recent years in computer algorithms and available data have the potential to further improve automated-scoring performance for existing

---

[10]Human scoring performance is typically used as the standard for evaluating the performance of automated scoring engines because it is the obvious alternative.

[11]See also Gregg, N., Young, M., and Lottridge, S. (2021, June). *Examining Fairness in Automated Scoring*, paper presented at the National Council on Measurement in Education, available in the project's Public Access File.

[12]Most of the work on group bias has been conducted on international university students who are non-native English speakers (Bridgeman, Trapani, and Attali, 2012; Burstein and Chodorow, 1999; Ramineni and Williamson, 2018).

[13]*2018 Auto Scoring Report in Reading, History, and Civics, Grades 4 and 8.* Internal NCES Report provided to the panel and available in the project's Public Access File.

and future item types (Ghosh, Klebanov, and Song, 2020; Mathias and Bhattacharyya, 2020; Riordan et al., 2020; Young et al., 2017). NAEP can expect to benefit from these improvements.

But these probable benefits come with complications. Using automated scoring would add another layer to the scoring process that requires technical oversight. It is also generally viewed with skepticism by the public (Wood, 2020), and it requires a program of validation to examine its effects on overall scoring and reporting. Careful planning related to technical oversight, public acceptance, and validation of its effects would be critical to the successful implementation of automated scoring. NAEP, given its national significance, is uniquely suited to leverage industry and academic expertise to lead the United States as an exemplar in how to incorporate automated scoring into an assessment program.

Evaluating Items for Feasibility of Automated Scoring

Automated scoring may not be appropriate for all NAEP items, for which a human-only scoring approach ("hand scoring") may be needed. The performance of current scoring engines varies across items across and within item types: that is, models may not meet performance criteria for all items (McGraw-Hill Education CTB, 2014). Recognizing this limitation, NCES was in the process of conducting an open challenge to compare the performance of multiple scoring engines on NAEP reading assessment items at the time this report was being completed.[14]

Factors that influence both engine and human ability to score items include the depth of knowledge assessed by the item, the number of elicited concepts and the nature of the relationship between those concepts, the degree of variation in how concepts are described by examinees, the level of alignment between the item and the rubric, whether items stand alone or have dependencies, and the clarity of the item prompt and rubric (DiCerbo, Lai, and Ventura, 2020; Leacock and Zhang, 2014; Leacock, Messineo, and Zhang, 2013; Lottridge, Wood, and Shaw, 2018; Raczynski, Choi, and Cohen, 2021). Consideration of these factors during item creation can result in items that can be scored more successfully by both humans and automated scoring engines. The degree to which humans can score with high quality and agree with one another is also a driver of the level of agreement between scoring engines and humans (Patz, Lottridge, and Boyer, 2019; Wind et al., 2017).

---

[14]See https://github.com/NAEP-AS-Challenge/info.

Time and Cost Savings

The addition of automated scoring in NAEP can reduce the number of responses being hand scored, thereby decreasing both scoring time and cost. However, automated scoring does come with its own costs. Engine-related costs include obtaining a high-quality hand-scored sample (typically double-scored and resolved), engine training and validation, engine setup fees, and per-response or per-test scoring fees (Topol, Olson, and Roeber, 2014). It is also important to consider that some hand-scoring activities will still need to be done, especially around developing the rubric and training scorers to use it, hand scoring a subset of responses to train the model and monitor its performance, and monitoring the overall pattern of scores over time. There also may be additional costs for recalibrating models, special studies on model performance, and the costs for replacing any other hand-scoring activities that occur beyond score assignment (e.g., plagiarism detection).

Although NAEP scores a lot of responses and has a lot of items, the number of responses per item is relatively low—ranging from 2,000 to 30,000 per item (NAEP, 2013). Items are included in test forms about four times, resulting in total response counts of 8,000 to 120,000 across the life of a typical item in main NAEP; items in long-term trend NAEP are used more times because they are unchanged for a longer period of time. Items in the mandated reading and mathematics assessments with state and urban district samples are at the top of the range of response counts: items used in assessments with national samples are at the bottom of this range. In most implementations, automated-scoring models are trained for every item, and so increasing items increases costs.[15] The NAEP response counts per item are near the threshold for achieving cost savings from automated scoring, which is typically around 30,000 responses; it depends on the cost savings from hand scoring and the overall number of items automatically scored.

Criteria for Examining Fairness and Validity Issues

The quality of automated-scoring procedures needs to be evaluated in the same ways as are done for human-scoring procedures (Bennett, 2011; Lottridge, Burkhardt, and Boyer, 2020; Williamson, Xi, and Breyer, 2012; Yan and Bridgeman, 2020). This evaluation should seek to determine the extent to which machine scores are reliable, fair, and valid for their intended

[15]The use of item models for item creation—as discussed in Chapter 4—may allow automated-scoring models to be trained at the model level, rather than for individual items, which could result in further cost savings. While generic scoring models across items have been implemented in some contexts, this approach would need to be compared with the rubric requirements to ensure that scoring is valid.

uses and the inferences they support. Studies will be needed to compare machine scores and hand scores in terms of descriptive statistics (i.e., mean, standard deviation, and distribution), rate of agreement between automated scores and human scores at the item level and the test level, and other measures of quality and to determine whether they vary with the training data used. These comparisons will need to be conducted for the full group of test takers and for test takers grouped by race and ethnicity, gender, English-learner status, disability status, family socioeconomic status, and other characteristics of interest.[16]

Fairness is a particularly important issue to consider in evaluations, given that research has documented disparities related to machine learning and automated scoring (Corbett-Davies and Goel, 2018; Hutchinson and Mitchell, 2019). The committee highlights the criteria established in Williamson, Xi, and Breyer (2012), which are widely used. Seeking to answer the question, "Is it fair to subgroups of interest to substitute a human grader with an automated score?," Williamson outlined several group differences to examine: differences in the associations between automated and human scores across groups at the task, task type, and reported score levels; differences in the generalizability of automated scores by group; differences in the predictive ability of automated scoring; and difference in relation to the decisions made based on the scores.[17] In evaluating fairness, it is also important to examine whether humans are introducing bias and, if so, to introduce methods to correct the bias, such as improved training and monitoring.

Finally, while the concepts of machine learning and automated scoring are becoming increasingly familiar to the public, there is still considerable skepticism. Much distrust rests on the fact that computers do not "understand" language in the way humans do and that the mechanisms underlying automated scoring do not match how humans score (Page, 2003; Wood, 2020). These are reasonable criticisms that programs using automated scoring need to address. Wood (2020) offers seven recommendations that focus on the creation of public-facing documentation that outlines how

---

[16]Guidance and criteria for evaluation procedures are available in several publications, including Lottridge, Burkhardt, and Boyer (2020); Williamson, Xi, and Breyer (2012); and Yan and Bridgeman (2020). A broader approach to evaluation is discussed by Bejar (2011) and Bennett (2011), both of which present the view that automated scoring procedures should not be judged in isolation, without considering other aspects of the test and the testing context.

[17]Other researchers suggest conducting differential item functioning analyses (Bridgeman, Trapani, and Attali, 2012; Shermis et al., 2017). If differences are identified, then it is important to investigate the source of those differences, both for human scorers and the engine (Ramineni and Williamson, 2018). See also Gregg, N., Young, M., and Lottridge, S. (2021, June), *Examining Fairness in Automated Scoring,* paper presented at the National Council on Measurement in Education, available in the project's Public Access File.

automated scoring works, how it is used in the program, and evidence of its performance, such as the results of comparisons with hand scoring. While NAEP does not report results at the examinee level, it is still critical to be able to explain the use of automated scoring to both technical and nontechnical audiences (Shermis and Lottridge, 2019).

ANTICIPATED COST REDUCTIONS FROM AUTOMATED SCORING

NCES currently plans to implement automated scoring where feasible for items in the reading and mathematics assessments in grades 4 and 8 in the near future.[18] These are the assessments with state-level samples that will provide sufficient responses over the four-test life of a typical item to make automated scoring cost effective.

Currently, 40 to 50 percent of the reading items and 25 percent of the mathematics items are hand scored.[19] NCES estimates that automated scoring can be used for 70 percent of the hand-scored reading items and 40 percent of the hand-scored mathematics items.[20] These figures are being empirically tested in the open challenge that is being conducted as this report is finalized and will be examined in future research studies.[21] For the items that use automated scoring, hand scoring will continue for about 5 to 10 percent of responses to monitor the performance of automated scoring.[22]

NCES estimates that automated scoring will cut the cost of hand scoring in half for the reading and mathematics assessments in grades 4 and 8 starting in fiscal 2024,[23] which would save approximately $2.5 million in scoring costs every 2 years. This reduction of $1.25 million in the annual average scoring cost represents 0.7 percent of NAEP's budget. NCES estimates that a transition to develop online NAEP and automated scoring would require an investment of $2.5 million.[24] This investment "include[s] proof of concept and field test studies for online administration in addition to special studies to examine the feasibility of automated scoring."[25]

---

[18]NCES response to Q57b.

[19]NCES response to Q57b.

[20]NCES response to Q57b.

[21]NCES (personal communication, December 17, 2021).

[22]NCES (personal communication, December 17, 2021).

[23]NCES response to Q57b.

[24]NCES (personal communication, January 14, 2022).

[25]NCES response to Q57a. The NCES response to Q78 provides further detail about this work: The proof of concept will cost $80,000 and will "evaluate the use of automated scoring to score 2017 release NAEP grade 4 and 8 reading items." A field test for $1–1.5 million will carry out a "duplicate 'Shadow Score' of 2019 NAEP Math & Reading items" using "the entire corpus of 285 constructed response mathematics and reading items." In addition, NCES referred to ongoing special studies involving human double scoring ($400,000–600,000 each)

As would be expected on the basis of the typical industry experience for the threshold for automated scoring to be cost effective, NCES projections imply that automated scoring will result in only modest net cost savings over the next few years.

The cost savings projected by NCES do not currently reflect any use of automated scoring on other assessments with large state-level samples. Automated scoring may not be cost effective for these assessments because the low frequency of these assessments may not generate enough responses for each item. It is quite unlikely that automated scoring would be cost effective for the assessments with only national-level samples.

RECOMMENDATION 7-1: The National Center for Education Statistics (NCES) should continue its work to implement automated scoring on the reading and mathematics assessments for grades 4 and 8, with the item types that current scoring engines can score accurately and consistently. NCES should also consider the use of automated scoring on other assessments administered to state-level samples. In addition to benefiting from modest net reductions in costs, NCES should work to leverage the potential of automated scoring to improve the speed of reporting, increase the information provided about open-ended responses, and increase the consistency and fairness of scoring over time.

---

that will monitor the accuracy of automated scoring and work to expand its use.

8

Analysis and Reporting

This chapter addresses innovations related to analysis and reporting. It begins by describing the relevant costs and then discusses several aspects of innovative analysis and reporting for NAEP. Arguably, all of NAEP's impact is mediated through its analysis and reporting procedures. As the primary mechanisms for communicating with the public, NAEP's reports need to clearly convey the results of an assessment. They also need to be released in a timely way and help the public understand the current achievement of U.S. students, as well as the trends in educational progress over time. This chapter focuses on score reporting and the supporting data and analyses.

CURRENT COSTS

The Alliance contract for design, analysis, and reporting has an estimated annual average cost of $17.6 million.[1] With an average of 5.5 assessments per year, the design, analysis, and reporting costs average $3.2 million per test. These costs are divided equally between design and analysis ("design, psychometric and statistical analysis") and reporting.[2]

Although the NAEP program periodically adopts innovations in design, analysis, and reporting, the approaches used tend to be broadly similar

[1]See Table 2-2 in Chapter 2. NCES response to Q33 says that the design, analysis, and reporting contract includes the following activities: "designs all pilot and field tests, operational assessments, and special studies; analyzes data ensuring reporting of valid results; proposes and prepares psychometric and statistical analyses compatible with previous NAEP methodologies; specifies data needed to meet the goals for reporting; and prepares reports."

[2]NCES response to Q32.

across assessments, changing slowly over time. These costs appear to be higher than comparable costs for other large assessments—which often have much smaller budgets overall—but the panel was not able to obtain good data for comparison.

NCES notes, however, that NAEP has special analysis and reporting costs that many other large assessment programs do not have.[3] With respect to design and analysis, NAEP has a mandate to describe trends, which can necessitate additional analyses to understand changes between assessments (such as the transition to digitally based assessments) or unusual periods (such as the first set of post-pandemic results). With respect to reporting, NAEP has a mandate to inform the public and make its results accessible, which includes developing multiple types of reports, carrying out high-profile press release events, and providing ready access to results from confidential data through the NAEP Data Explorer.[4]

INNOVATIVE ANALYSIS AND REPORTING

Substantial innovations in analysis and reporting have taken place over the past several decades, some specific to NAEP and others that are more general. On the analysis side, complex analyses that were previously specially programmed are now largely automated. This includes, for example, the analyses carried out to understand the performance of items and to populate the standardized "report card" reports.[5] In addition, NAEP pioneered the provision of customized online analyses, with the NAEP Data Explorer, though the platform limits data elements and visualizations, which reduces its potential use for educational research.[6]

Another innovative aspect of data analyses concerns the use of process data, based on the data stream created by student interactions with computer-based testing. Analyses of these data have been a major contributor to new academic disciplines, such as learning analytics and educational data mining (Romero and Ventura, 2020). For example, research on other programs has investigated the extent to which process data predict constructs like student persistence and self-regulated learning (Roll and Winne, 2015). Leading scholars in educational measurement have also identified the potential use of these data to improve understanding of student knowledge (e.g., Mislevy, 2019).

NCES has played a leading role in making NAEP process data available for research and supporting work to develop its use (Center for Process Data, n.d.; Circi et al., 2020; Nation's Report Card, n.d.). A recent

---

[3]NCES response to Q77.

[4]See https://nces.ed.gov/nationsreportcard/tdw/database/data_tool.asp.

[5]NCES response to Q77.

[6]Expanding the Data Explorer's functionality would require addressing issues of confidentiality and student privacy, in addition to other technical issues.

synthesis provides an overview of how process data have been used historically in scoring NAEP items and how they could be used to deepen understanding about test-taker responses (Bergner and von Davier, 2019). Extensive research has been conducted by NAEP Alliance contractors and external researchers using NAEP process data, which has shown that these data can provide important information for forensics, integrity, and higher-order processes, such as scoring and scaling (Provasnik, 2021). Moving forward, interaction data during pilot testing could be used to determine item validity. In addition, feedback could be provided to proctors in real time, enabling them to identify students who might be disengaged and prompt them to return their focus to NAEP.

With respect to reporting, NAEP score reports have regularly provided high-level overviews of NAEP results. Recently, NAEP has used standardization and is considering potential use of artificial intelligence to speed the release of the initial "report card" reports for assessments, as well as shortening the time for making data available from 1 year to 6 months.[7] Reports that analyze relationships between NAEP data and other variables are consistently among the most popular reports produced by NAEP.[8] However, there are relatively few such reports, in large part because NAEP's mission does not explicitly focus on producing such analytical reports to inform policy in the way that the Organisation for Economic Co-operation and Development and some other agencies do.[9] This constraint underlines the importance to NAEP's mission of making its data available to others and ensuring that those data provide support for the kinds of analyses that would be useful for policy, particularly with respect to inequities across groups.

Thinking broadly, there are at least three ways that the availability of NAEP data could be improved:

1. Speed: To encourage analyses by outside researchers, NAEP could make its data available more quickly to allow those analyses to take place. One way to do this would be to create a select pool of researchers who have access to NAEP's raw data under embargo before their release to foster the development of policy-relevant analyses to appear shortly after release.
2. Accessibility: To encourage wider and more innovative use of NAEP data among researchers, journalists, and policy makers,

---

[7]NCES response to Q41.

[8]NCES response to Q43.

[9]NCES response to Q45: "NAEP is also administered by a federal statistical agency [NCES] and adheres to accepted policies which prohibit the mixing of official statistics and policy analysis."

the limited functionality of the NAEP Data Explorer could be expanded to make it easier to use and with more sophisticated analytic capabilities.

3. Depth: To support deeper analyses of NAEP's innovative items, the program could expand the availability and use of its process data. To support deeper analyses of NAEP's identification of inequities across groups, the program could expand the availability and use of important contextual variables to help identify plausible hypotheses about those inequities.

NAEP exists in a wide ecosystem of assessments and data. Already, advanced technologies—and what used to be advanced but now are commonplace technologies—are being applied widely across consumer and industrial platforms. These technologies raise users' expectations of what is available and how it appears. For example, people now expect to be able to find things easily through internet searches and to access databases that are interactive, customizable, and potentially even adaptive to the user over time. In this ecosystem, there is substantial scope for innovations in the approach to analysis and reporting that can more effectively use the program's substantial analysis and reporting budget to improve the insights that are generated from NAEP's data.

RECOMMENDATION 8-1: The National Center for Education Statistics should devote a greater percentage of its budget for innovative analysis and reporting that will increase the use and understanding of NAEP's data, including finding ways to make the raw data available more quickly to researchers, improving the usability and sophistication of the NAEP Data Explorer, making process data more easily accessible, and expanding the availability and use of important contextual variables.

9

Technological Infrastructure

This chapter addresses the technological infrastructure that is essential to developing, administering, analyzing, and reporting an assessment in the modern era. This infrastructure is obviously critical to many of the potential innovations discussed in this report. The chapter begins with a short overview of NAEP's current technology costs and investments and then describes a vision of the functionality that a fully developed technological infrastructure can provide. The last section discusses the development status of Next-Gen eNAEP, which will provide the next generation of the program's technology platform.

CURRENT COSTS

Technology is covered by two contracts in the NAEP Alliance, one for the web and the other for platform development.[1] The estimated annual average cost is $10.2 million for the web contract and $19.2 million for

[1]NCES response to Q33: The "web/technology development, operations and management" contract covers the following activities: "Develops, implements, and supports Internet-related applications and services; identifies and deploys emerging technologies and new products to improve NAEP's web and other computer-based products and services; monitors compliance with all NCES web requirements, and ensures timely release of quality products and services using Web technologies." The "NAEP platform development" contract covers the following activities: "Develops NAEP assessment delivery platform utilizing a state-of-the-art, age-appropriate user interface (UI) and overall user experience (UX) that is consistent, intuitive, and accessible across all subjects and grade levels."

the platform development contract.[2] The platform development contract is roughly evenly divided between development of the new system and maintenance (initially maintenance of the old eNAEP system and later maintenance of the new Next-Gen eNAEP system).

VISION FOR A TECHNOLOGICAL INFRASTRUCTURE FOR NAEP

Exploratory research in psychometrics using data science, machine learning, and artificial intelligence provides a vision of a future in which assessments are much more flexible, adaptable, and integrated into a student's learning experiences than current assessments (Markowetz et al., 2014; Romero and Ventura, 2020; von Davier et al., 2019). The above chapters have already covered some of the capabilities that could be included in such an approach to assessment, including model-driven and fully automated item generation (Chapter 4), the administration of assessment on a wide variety of devices (Chapter 5), adaptive testing (Chapter 6), automated scoring of constructed responses (Chapter 7), and the analysis of process data (Chapter 8).

To support a full range of innovations—those that should be implemented now and those that will become compelling in a decade or more—NAEP needs a robust technology platform that is flexible enough to incorporate a series of innovations as they become ready for application. These potential innovations span the full chain of the NAEP program, including test design, item and test development, test administration, scoring, analysis of results, and reporting.

A robust data architecture for NAEP needs to integrate data flows, support quality control and other analysis processes, and provide easy and secure access to historical NAEP data. At present, NAEP data are held in separate silos, each administered by a different Alliance contractor, which prevents NCES staff from directly accessing data outside of pre-defined data products. For any new kind of analysis, additional requests and review are required, which impedes new analytical studies and more integrated use of data. This situation can make it prohibitively expensive and slow to implement psychometric innovations that are based on response data, such as adaptive testing, automated scoring, adaptive reporting, and other operational implementations of advanced algorithms. By reducing the manual merging, integration, and analysis of data files, NAEP can become more efficient and reduce the effort needed for administration.

Contemporary data architectures provide an elegant and effective solution to these issues, with secured authentication systems providing access application programming interface endpoints in a standardized manner by any technology application. This new architecture could provide the

[2]See Table 2-2 in Chapter 2.

foundation for NAEP to successfully integrate innovations from artificial intelligence, assessment engineering, and other advances in ways that have been very difficult to incorporate in the past. If such a system is not pursued, it could block the successful modernization of NAEP and require ongoing large investments to provide ongoing basic functionality and stability.

The field of software development has generally moved over the past several decades toward leveraging the benefits that come from using standards-based approaches and interoperable systems. These approaches have generally been accepted in the field as having substantial benefits for reducing errors and costs related to software development. These common industry practices include

- Standards-based development: the use of industry standards, such as IMS QTI[3] for item structure and xAPI[4] for process data format, increases the speed of development and enables integration with other systems and analysis.
- Cloud-based technology systems: the use of cloud native platforms, such as Amazon Web Services or Microsoft Azure, can provide the foundation for increased interoperability in a distributed system, as well as improved services and reduced cost. This is likely to be true for NAEP, for which the small annual assessment window makes it attractive to have an infrastructure system that can be "turned off" when not in use.
- Federated architecture: an assessment architecture based on a "system of systems" principle, linked together through these protocols and data security standards, enables new systems and technologies to be added as they become available.

These new and now common practices suggest important staffing considerations in developing such systems. It is unclear whether these considerations are reflected in NCES's current staffing plans and contract arrangements. The expertise needed to lead a large-scale psychometric software development of this kind is distinctly different from the expertise needed to develop assessment items, administer an assessment, or analyze its results, which all rely on the resulting technology infrastructure. But using the infrastructure is different than creating it. The expertise needed for the software development for the technology architecture includes

- experience with cloud-based architectures and software development;

[3]See https://www.imsglobal.org/question/index.html.
[4]See https://sagroups.ieee.org/9274-1-1/.

- psychometric processes and data standards for assessment items; and
- agile-based and customer-responsive software development.

DEVELOPMENT OF THE NEXT-GEN ENAEP PLATFORM[5]

The platform and technology approach of the current eNAEP system is almost a decade old and is based on a custom application using dedicated tablet computers, dedicated internet routers, and technical staff at every school that participates in NAEP. The dedicated tablets are only used during the administration of NAEP and other NCES surveys; they are unused for the rest of the year. As described in Chapter 5, this approach reduces school burden, provides absolute consistency in appearance of and interaction with test items, and does not require any reliance on school connectivity. However, it is very expensive and no longer necessary for schools that now routinely administer high-stakes assessments using local computers.

The current contract for NAEP platform development funds the development of Next-Gen eNAEP, a multistage development activity that is planned through 2024. This new system includes not only an assessment delivery platform application for students, but also a library of reusable item components, a "data lake" to store all current and historical NAEP data, and mechanisms for data access with a commitment to extensibility, reusability, and other contemporary software design principles. The current contract goes through 2024 and includes a field test for online administration using NAEP-owned devices in 2023 and a proof-of-concept study for delivering NAEP on school-owned devices in 2024.[6] An operational system is a deliverable of the current contract, and Next-Gen eNAEP will be used for both the pilot and operational NAEP administrations in 2024.[7] After 2024, the system will be used to deliver NAEP on school-owned devices in a field test in 2025 and then for an operational test in 2026.

The panel was provided documentation that describes the goals, vision, and roadmap to develop Next-Gen eNAEP. However, these materials do not provide the detail needed to understand the underlying technical approaches. In addition, much of the documentation provided focuses on test delivery, so it is unclear how much functionality will initially be provided related to item authoring and test assembly, scoring, reporting, data architectures, and data access.

---

[5]After a prepublication version of the report was provided to Institute of Education Sciences, NCES, and NAGB, this section was edited to revise the descriptions of the capabilities of the Next-Gen eNAEP platform, the timeline for its use in operational administrations, and the expertise of the NCES staff who oversee its development.

[6]NCES responses to panel questions (personal communication, August 11, 2021).

[7]NCES response to Q73c.

An operating assumption from NCES is that item appearance should not change between the current and the new system, out of concern about potential threats to item validity and trend. Therefore, the new system incorporates the presentation layer from the current eNAEP while replacing the back-end data infrastructure, item rendering, and other components. However, as discussed in Chapter 5, some variance is inevitable with the use of multiple machines and browsers, and only a basic level of compatibility can be guaranteed in any software development activity. Recommendation 5-2 (in Chapter 5) proposes that the program should plan to accommodate this inevitable variance by collecting data on the systems used at different sites and then reflecting any differences in the analysis. This approach opens up potential flexibility in the item appearance requirements for Next-Gen eNAEP.

The custom building of enterprise software for a single program is an expensive approach, in terms of both initial development and delivery and later maintenance on an ongoing basis. The amount budgeted in the current contract for this activity through fiscal 2024 (roughly $50 million) is an indicator of the cost implications of this approach. By building a new system internally, NCES does not leverage the cost sharing that occurs in standard commercial development, in which a component developed serves multiple customers who effectively share the cost, whether explicitly or indirectly. NCES informed the panel that no current system met the full requirements when the current direction was defined, and this approach enables the ultimate control in terms of functionality and requirements.[8] However, this choice requires that NAEP spend whatever it takes every time a new functionality, defect fix, or other maintenance update is required.

Given the dynamism in the field of software development, it is likely that the options available to NCES for both building and buying the relevant components of eNAEP are substantially different than they were when the decision was made to develop the system in-house. Fortunately, the platform development contract includes research and business analysis of other technologies to "stay continually abreast of the latest trends and innovations in large-scale assessment and education technology."[9] As part of this work, it is important to be clear that many vendors have successfully administered K–12 summative assessments using platforms that are based on the kinds of software tools and standards specified by NAEP.

RECOMMENDATION 9-1: The National Center for Education Statistics (NCES) should regularly evaluate the software built by vendors or available in open-source libraries for its potential to meet the

[8]NCES response to Q73e.

[9]NCES response to Q73e.

requirements of the different components of Next-Gen eNAEP. To support the viability of local administration of NAEP, the ease of installing, managing, and troubleshooting test delivery software should be a strong consideration in selecting the software to be used. Given the substantial ongoing expense associated with developing and maintaining a proprietary platform, Next-Gen eNAEP components should be custom built only if there are clearly large net benefits from doing so that have been identified by rigorous analysis. This decision should be made on a component basis, not as a single decision to build or buy all components. NCES should immediately carry out an evaluation with respect to any components of Next-Gen eNAEP that have not already been substantially developed, and then periodically thereafter. The platform development contract should provide the right incentives to make the best decision between building and buying each component.

The NAEP Alliance member selected to perform this activity is a global leader in psychometric research and development and is not known in the field for development of production enterprise software applications and assessment technology platforms. The planning documents provided to the panel reference best-of-breed approaches to software development using agile planning, cloud-native technologies, extensible and modular code, and other approaches. NCES also reports that the Alliance member has been meeting the deliverable schedule and meeting expectations.[10]

Although NCES staff have some experience in planning enterprise software development, it will be critical that NCES have additional technical staff expertise to provide oversight and guidance for the development of a project of this magnitude. Staff should have the background required to evaluate alternative technical approaches, review requirements for testing components of the system, and inspect testing of software components. Guidance in cloud-based applications, data infrastructure systems, and psychometrics will be needed to ensure that the system performs as needed and can move NAEP to the next generation. NCES reported to the panel that it is consulting regularly with NAEP's Digital Transition Advisory Council and the State Education Technology Director's Association, but it is highly likely that additional technical resources will be needed.[11]

The technical expertise may be a challenge for NCES given that most staff have either psychometric or statistical backgrounds but do not have this technical background. Given the criticality of this system to achieve program goals and cost reduction, it will be important to find staff who

[10]NCES response to Q73b and to follow-up questions (personal communication, August 11, 2021).

[11]NCES response to Q73e.

can fulfill this role. These resources need to have regular review and input into the development of the software.

RECOMMENDATION 9-2: The National Center for Education Statistics (NCES) should ensure that there is adequate internal and external expertise related to enterprise software development to support and oversee the development of Next-Gen eNAEP for both the NCES staff and for staff working for the platform development contractor. This software expertise is substantially different than expertise related to psychometrics and statistics.

An open question is the appropriateness of the budget for this system. The panel was provided a rough breakdown of the current platform development contract between the cost of maintaining the current system, developing the Next-Gen platform, and future maintenance of the new system.[12] Yet the NCES reports indicate that most changes will be enhancements to the existing system. Given the high-level functional descriptions provided and overlap between old and new systems, the panel was not able to evaluate the correspondence between the functional descriptions and the deliverables. In addition, the panel itself does not have sufficient expertise related to enterprise software development to evaluate whether the estimated annual average budget of $19.2 million is appropriate for the development plan.

RECOMMENDATION 9-3: The National Center for Education Statistics should seek expert guidance from enterprise application developers and educational technologists who understand assessment technology platforms to evaluate the reasonability of the projected costs for the development of Next-Gen eNAEP.

[12]NCES response to Q73c.

10

Program Management, Planning, Support, and Oversight[1]

This chapter addresses NAEP's overall program management, planning, support, and oversight functions. These functions include a wide array of tasks that are important to the program but not directly related to specific assessment components: defining the program's direction; overseeing and coordinating the staff, contractors, stakeholder representatives, and experts who guide and implement the program; and carrying out the necessary planning functions to define innovations in the program and coordinate existing work. The planning functions related to innovation often involve some research and development, which are included with the overall management costs. Program management, planning, support, and oversight includes the functions played by NAGB and NCES staff, by NAGB members, by the many participants in NAEP stakeholder and expert advisory groups, and by many Alliance contractors.

Program management, planning, support, and oversight are not an explicit focus of the panel's statement of task (see Chapter 1), though it is mentioned in its call for "*programmatic changes and research* needed for NAEP to explore innovations while balancing the competing objectives of cost reduction, technical quality and informative value" [emphasis added]. The panel initially considered these functions in precisely the supporting role suggested by the statement of task. However, after reviewing the program's overall cost structure, the panel concluded that potential reductions

[1]After a prepublication version of the report was provided to Institute of Education Sciences (IES), NCES, and NAGB, this chapter was edited to reflect a broader range of costs and to revise the description and estimate of the costs associated with the non-support contracts.

in the cost of program management, planning, support, and oversight functions would play a critical role in any cost reduction strategy for NAEP.

The members of the panel were chosen with a view to address a request focused on assessment and potential technological innovation, not a request focused on organizational reengineering. As a result, we have limited our discussion of these issues to areas for which the panel members are familiar with relevant literature. As our recommendation below indicates, this topic needs further attention.

After discussing the costs related to program management, planning, support, and oversight, the chapter briefly discusses the importance of taking a systemic approach to the overall design of the program and considering the role of research and innovation in the program.

CURRENT COSTS

The cost of NAEP program management, planning, support, and oversight is divided across a number of different budgets and contracts and is therefore hard to understand. These costs are of three different types:

1. Federal program staff: The direct and indirect costs related to the federal government employees who staff the NAGB and NCES program offices for NAEP are not separately identified in appropriations. Overall, there are roughly 32 federal employees who primarily support NAEP for either NAGB[2] or NCES. Table 2-2 (in Chapter 2) provides an estimated annual average cost for these staff of $7.1 million.[3]
2. NAEP support contracts: NAEP includes several different contracts that provide various sorts of management and support functions. In the NAEP contract summaries provided by NCES, these contracts are identified as program management support or support contracts, with estimated annual average costs of $6.2 million and $37.0 million, respectively.[4]

[2]As a legislatively established independent entity within the Department of Education, NAGB's annual appropriation is uniquely set up as separate line item within the IES budget. The appropriation does not segregate salaries and expenses from all other costs. The annual appropriation, $7.1 million in fiscal 2021 for example, covers not only salaries and expenses, office rent, and contract costs, but all other aspects of NAGB's operations as an independent entity. NAGB (personal communication, March 15, 2022).

[3]This figure underestimates the cost for NCES staff by including only salaries.

[4]NCES response to Q33: The "program support management" contract covers the following activities: "Manages the NAEP program in alignment with Project Management (PM) best practices to ensure proper scheduling, quality control, risk management and communication across contractors and handoffs." The "support contract" category actually includes several different contracts over the years that have been combined for the historical analysis under

3. Costs within the non-support contracts that reflect various aspects of management, planning, and oversight.

The panel was not able to obtain sufficient details of these program-related costs in relation to the various staff and contractor activities. No doubt, some of these costs reflect the complex governance arrangement for the NAEP program, and some reflect the complex design of the Alliance contracts.

The panel also does not have good estimates of the relevant costs across the non-support contracts. Based on the very limited information we have available, these costs are plausibly at least in the range of 10 to 15 percent of the respective budgets.[5] Spread across the $125 million of non-support contracts, that range would suggest potential additional costs of $12.5 to $18.8 million.

Overall, the panel roughly estimates the cost of program management, planning, support, and oversight for NAEP from these first two types of costs—federal staff and support contracts—is about $50.3 million or about 28.7 percent of the total budget for NAEP. Related costs in the non-support contracts might add substantially more. While acknowledging the complexity and importance of NAEP, the panel thinks these costs are very large, both in absolute terms and as a percentage of the overall NAEP budget. Meaningful cost reduction for the NAEP program will need to include a consideration of potential reduction of these costs.

TAKING A SYSTEMIC APPROACH TO DESIGNING ASSESSMENT PROGRAMS

Large-scale assessment programs like NAEP are complex endeavors, involving many activities, including test development, psychometrics, and reporting. Each activity is highly technical and operationally challenging. The integration and implementation of all the activities is even more complex and challenging. The assessment community has a groundbreaking stream of research looking at systemic approaches to assessment design, going under such labels as "evidence-centered design" (Mislevy, 2006; Mislevy, Steinberg, and Almond, 2003), "assessment engineering" (Luecht, 2012a, 2012b, 2020a, 2020b; Luecht and Burke, 2020), and, more generically, "principled approaches" (Ferrara et al., 2017). The NAEP program

the label of "planning and coordination" (NCES response to Q72a) and cover the following activities: "Ensures coordination among Alliance contractors; maintains data for tracking program progress; and provides logistical support for complaints and substantive comments."

[5]The planning portion of the item development contract is in this range (NCES, personal communication, March 15, 2022).

is already capitalizing on some of this literature, and we recommend that more be done along these lines.

However, the complexity of NAEP's assessment activities is further compounded by the program's organizational structure: separate federal agencies responsible for the program's policies and administration, and implementation of the assessment program by a complex team of contractors. This organizational complexity comes from a clear logic: two agencies to play two different roles, and a contract structure that allows separate companies with expertise in different areas to bid on the work in areas for which they have expertise. However, this seemingly logical structure then produces predictable overlaps and inefficiencies in a program in which decisions about one activity can have implications for all the other activities. This produces the set of review bodies and advisory committees noted in Chapter 2. In caricature: everyone who is involved with one part of NAEP needs to review everything else related to NAEP and to keep up with everyone else's reviews.

The costs related to this organizational structure need to be addressed systemically. The kind of systemic thinking that NCES is applying to assessment design needs to be applied to the complexity of NAEP's organizational structure. The high cost of NAEP program management, planning, support, and oversight affects every other part of the assessment.

The panel is only slightly familiar with other research literatures that call for systemic thinking for solving organizational problems. For example, Steiber (2014) lists a systems approach as one of the six key management principles for successful, continuously innovating firms. Although this panel is not constituted to conduct a thorough evaluation of the organizational structures that give rise to such costs for program management, planning, support, and oversight, it is clear that the challenge of NAEP's costs cannot be addressed by looking only at the activities that directly relate to developing, administering, and reporting on the assessments.

RECOMMENDATION 10-1: The National Assessment Governing Board and the National Center for Education Statistics should commission an independent audit of the program management and decision-making processes and costs in the NAEP program, with a charge and sufficient access to review the program's costs in detail. That audit should include proposed ways to streamline these processes.

The activities that are grouped together under program management, planning, support, and oversight include many of the research activities that are carried out to support the planning process. This research provides the basis for launching the development of new innovations and monitoring their progress and impact as they are implemented. Examples include studies related to specific topics addressed in this report, such as computer-based delivery, automated item generation, automated scoring, and the development of eNAEP.

Strikingly, however, there is no way for the panel, or anyone else, to see an integrated summary of these research activities with respect to both their cost and their coverage and vision. This absence is particularly noteworthy given the role NAEP seeks to play as an exemplar for other assessment programs: those other assessment programs could benefit substantially from understanding the kinds of innovations NAEP has identified to explore and the lessons the program has learned from those explorations. And the absence is particularly striking in considering the task that faced this panel to provide advice on valuable innovations for NAEP to consider for the years ahead.

RECOMMENDATION 10-2: The National Center for Education Statistics should increase the visibility and coherence of NAEP's research activities to help NAEP's stakeholders, as well as other assessment programs, understand the innovations the program is investigating and the lessons it is learning. The NAEP research program should have an identifiable budget and program of activities.

Such a research program might include research related to evaluation, validity, innovative assessment items, and new assessment technologies.

11

Summary: A New Path for NAEP

NAEP is unique in the information it provides, but it is also very expensive and increasingly so. NAEP assessments are roughly twice as expensive as the assessments of the Program for International Student Assessment (PISA) and a full order of magnitude more expensive than almost all high-stakes state assessments. While the increases in NAEP's costs have been accompanied by important expansions in the information made available to users, the program's high cost raises concern about its long-term viability.

Encouraged by recent innovations in assessment technology that are increasingly used in state K–12 testing and other large-scale assessment programs, NAEP's leaders are exploring their feasibility for use with NAEP. Of interest is the extent to which these innovations might reduce costs while maintaining or enhancing technical quality. The work of this panel is to contribute to that exploration by providing analysis and recommendations for the next phase of NAEP. This chapter summarizes our recommendations: taken together, they chart an ambitious yet practical way for the National Center for Education Statistics and the National Assessment Governing Board to plan for NAEP's future.

CLARIFYING AND DETAILING NAEP'S COSTS

To carry out its task, the panel needed to obtain information about NAEP's costs, in order to put the potential value of possible cost savings in context. As detailed throughout the report, particularly in Chapter 2, and despite cooperation from NCES, the panel could not obtain a clear picture of the overall budget for NAEP and how it is spent for the program's different functions.

RECOMMENDATION 2-1: The National Center for Education Statistics and the National Assessment Governing Board should develop clear, consistent, and complete descriptions of current spending on the major components of NAEP, including contract structure, contractual spending, and direct spending on government staff and other costs. These cost descriptions should be used to inform major decisions about the program to ensure that their long-term budgetary impact is supportable.

CHANGING THE WAY TRENDS ARE MONITORED AND REPORTED

In the core subjects of mathematics and reading, NAEP has two assessment programs for measuring educational progress. One program, long-term trend NAEP, tracks trends since the 1970s and uses some test questions that are largely unchanged since NAEP's beginnings. The other program, main NAEP, has tracked achievement since 1990. Main NAEP's testing frameworks are reviewed and refreshed every 10 years or so.

NAEP currently reports both long-term trend data and main NAEP data for reading and mathematics. While this can be confusing to users, long-term trend NAEP complements the information provided by main NAEP and brings a useful balance to the NAEP portfolio. In addition, in light of the COVID-19 pandemic, long-term trend NAEP will provide a useful gauge to measure trends before and after the pandemic and provide information about the possible inequities that marked instruction during that period. However, long-term trend NAEP needs to be modernized to maintain its relevance and it is an open question whether its ongoing value will justify the costs of modernization.

RECOMMENDATION 3-1: The National Center for Education Statistics should prepare a detailed plan and budget for the modernization of long-term trend NAEP, including the costs of creating post-hoc assessment frameworks, bridging between paper and digital assessment, maintaining trends, and ongoing costs after the bridge. Congress, the National Assessment Governing Board, and the National Center for Education Statistics should then consider the value of a modernized and continued long-term trend NAEP in comparison with other program priorities. If continued, long-term trend NAEP should be renamed to better distinguish it from the trend data provided by main NAEP.

For the more comprehensive trend information provided by main NAEP, the program could benefit from small, more frequent changes to the assessment frameworks, potentially for every administration. There are three ways to revise the process. First, more frequent framework updates could encourage the identification of smaller changes that are needed. Second, the use of a standing framework committee with rotating membership, rather than the appointment of a new committee for each framework update, could serve to establish a group with a commitment to continuity and evolution. Third, better integrating the work of the framework and item development committees would allow content experts and item authors to iteratively and seamlessly inform each other's work.

RECOMMENDATION 3-2: The National Assessment Governing Board (NAGB) and the National Center for Education Statistics (NCES) should work both independently and collaboratively to implement smaller and more frequent framework updates. This work should include consideration of the possibility of broadening the remit of the standing subject-matter committees that already exist to include responsibility for gradual framework updates, participation in item model development, and working directly with both NAGB and NCES.

INTEGRATING ASSESSMENTS FOR SUBJECTS WITH OVERLAPPING CONTENT

Since its beginning, NAEP has assessed subjects separately from one another. However, modern educational practice, as illustrated by the recent assessments adopted by many states, offers compelling arguments for combining assessments that test complementary subject matter, such as reading and writing or science and technology and engineering literacy. Such combined assessments could continue to report subscores for the subjects that have heretofore been assessed separately. Some items might do double duty and contribute to both subscores.

The upfront investment costs to develop the combined assessments might be substantial, but they may be outweighed by the savings realized from reducing the number of assessments. The downside of not actively considering assessments for combined subjects is illustrated by the cost pressures that force some subjects to be assessed infrequently, such as writing, or to have been effectively eliminated, such as economics and geography.

RECOMMENDATION 3-3: The National Assessment Governing Board should give high priority to consideration of integrating nonmandated subjects that are currently assessed separately (such as science and technology and engineering literacy), as well as the possibility

of integrated pairs of subjects that include a mandated subject, such as reading and writing. This consideration should examine the possibility of preserving separate subject subscores in an integrated assessment that could maintain trends, along with potential benefits related to efficiency and cost, closer alignment with student learning, and synergy across subjects that has been found by research.

UPDATING THE ITEM DEVELOPMENT PROCESS

The estimated average annual cost for the NAEP item development contract is \$16.3 million, which is 9.3 percent of NAEP's budget. Item development for NAEP is extremely expensive, and the reasons for these costs are unclear. NAEP develops about 600 new items a year at an average cost per item of roughly \$3,700 for item creation and \$36,500 for pilot testing. These costs are much higher than the item development costs of other testing programs on a per item basis; nevertheless, they represent only 2.5 percent of NAEP's budget. The lack of clarity about the remaining spending in this contract is concerning since it represents 6.8 percent of NAEP's budget.

RECOMMENDATION 4-1: The National Center for Education Statistics should examine the costs and scope of work in the item development contract that are not directly related to item development and pilot administration and explore possibilities for changes that would reduce costs.

Automated and Structured Item Development

Automatic item generation refers to the use of artificial intelligence and computer-based algorithms to automate some or all of the work of item development. This approach can lead to cost savings for assessments that predominantly use traditional multiple-choice item formats, particularly when the number of items is large. Although NAEP includes some of these types of items, their numbers are insufficient to justify the costs of implementing automatic item generation. In addition, it is difficult to use automatic item generation for the scenario-based and other complex item types that predominate in main NAEP. Though long-term trend NAEP uses larger numbers of traditional multiple-choice questions, this program develops few new items. As automatic item generation technologies evolve, however, it may be worthwhile to revisit their applicability for NAEP.

Although the current state of the art in automatic item generation has limited applicability to NAEP, recent advancements in the use of assessment design and engineering principles could be beneficial. Previous expert panels have recommended evidence-centered design principles for NAEP, and NCES is carrying out work along these lines. Previous panels have also suggested that item development begin with NAEP's achievement-level descriptions and cut scores and that these should drive the evidence claims that describe students' knowledge and skills and define their proficiency levels. The task models that result and guide item development will benefit the work of both the subject-matter experts who work with NAGB on framework development and item review and the NCES contractors who develop the items. The quality control and pilot testing efforts that now focus on individual items could shift to the task models and bring efficiencies to item development.

RECOMMENDATION 4-2: The National Assessment Governing Board and the National Center for Education Statistics should move toward using more structured processes for item development to both decrease costs and improve quality. This work should include drawing from the detailed achievement-level descriptions to specify intended inferences and claims, better integrating the work of framework development and item creation, and carrying out critical aspects of review and quality control at the level of task models rather than at the level of individual items.

Changing the Mix of Item Types

NAEP currently uses a range of item types, including selected-response items, constructed-response items, and scenario-based tasks. Item types are typically aligned with cognitive and content specifications such that more complex item types are used to assess more complex skills. This alignment need not be the case, however. Research and practice demonstrate that selected-response or simple constructed-response items can be used to assess cognitively complex material.

Changing the mix of item types could potentially change NAEP's average costs for item creation, pilot testing, test administration, and scoring. The average costs of the three item types are $1,750 for selected-response items, $2,500 for constructed-response items, and $13,000 for items that are part of scenario-based tasks. Given these differences, increasing the proportion of scenario-based items would increase item development costs, and increasing the proportion of selected-response items would decrease item development costs. There are likely similar relationships with respect to test administration and scoring costs.

RECOMMENDATION 4-3: The National Assessment Governing Board should commission an analysis of the value and cost of different

item types when multiple item types can measure the construct of interest. A full range of potential item types should be included in this analysis. The analysis should develop a framework for considering the tradeoff between value and cost. The value considered should include both the item's contribution to a score and its signal about the relevant components of the construct. The costs considered should include item development (both item creation and pilot administration), administration time, and scoring.

MODERNIZING NAEP ADMINISTRATION

The current NAEP administration model relies on professionally trained NAEP staff and contractors who travel to schools to administer the assessment. When NAEP transitioned to digitally based assessment, NCES provided the technology needed for students to test. This was intended to reduce the burden on schools while maintaining the level of standardization that is deemed essential for NAEP. It also helped ensure that the assessment could be given in all schools, even those with limited bandwidth and technology resources. This model is laborious, expensive, and unusual in comparison with the administration approach used for typical state assessments. Because it represents about 28.6 percent of NAEP's budget, test administration presents one of the clearest opportunities for cost savings.

NCES has outlined a plan to transition to locally based administration in which school staff would serve as proctors and students would use the school's equipment for the NAEP assessment. NCES refers to this change as a transition to "contactless administration" because NAEP staff would no longer be directly in charge of administering the test. NCES is also considering an intermediate "reduced contact" model in which NAEP staff would support test administration virtually without being physically present in each school where the test is given. NCES recognizes that it may have to provide equipment and proctors to some schools.

RECOMMENDATION 5-1: The National Center for Education Statistics (NCES) should continue to develop its plan to administer NAEP using local school staff as proctors with online assessment delivery on local school computers, with development and bridge studies as needed to understand the feasibility and effects of this change in different contexts. This new model should be accompanied by adequate training and support of school staff, including tailored support for schools with more limited resources that may need NCES to provide proctors and equipment. NCES should also explore the use of flexible administration windows to allow schools to develop plans that accommodate local constraints on available equipment and consider appropriate ways to

compensate local schools for their contributions to the administration, especially during the transition to this new model.

The move to local test administration assumes that NAEP will develop some minimum specifications for the equipment, operating systems, and connectivity that are needed. Despite this initial effort at standardization, there is likely to be considerable variability among the devices that meet the minimum specifications. Some level of variability is unavoidable: it reflects both the practical reality of using local devices and the necessary customization that allows students to use devices that are familiar to them. Accounting for this variability will be important in the analysis of the assessment results. To carry out these analyses, the program will need to collect detailed information from the testing sites about the equipment and operating systems that are used.

RECOMMENDATION 5-2: Since a key component of moving to local administration will be the development of minimum requirements for equipment, operating systems, and connectivity, information about local devices, bandwidth, and administration conditions will have to be included in the data collection. Analysts should use statistical techniques that account for the effects of differences in devices and other local conditions to produce estimates that generalize across those differences. The National Center for Education Statistics should explore the use of random effects and other statistical techniques to produce estimates that reflect generalization across devices.

NCES plans to begin a transition to local administration of the reading and mathematics assessments in 2026. NCES has recently estimated the cost savings associated with this change of $56 million from 2026 to 2030. The panel's analysis suggests that the potential savings may be substantially larger, perhaps as large as an annual average savings of roughly $30.8 million, or 18.7 percent of NAEP's current budget.

RECOMMENDATION 5-3: The National Center for Education Statistics (NCES) should review its estimates of the potential cost savings from local administration of the mandated assessments in reading and mathematics in grades 4 and 8. The estimated savings are unexpectedly small when local administration would largely eliminate the large current costs for traveling proctors and equipment, even after considering any offsetting additional costs for training and technological infrastructure. NCES should also consider the use of the local administration model for reducing costs of all other assessments, as well as the costs for the pilot administration of new items.

Testing Two Unrelated Subjects for Each Student

Another way of decreasing administration costs is to gather more information from each sampled student by increasing the number of questions each one answers. NCES is considering a plan for administering two subjects to each student for the mandated assessments in reading and mathematics, a plan that we endorse.

Currently, each student takes two blocks of test questions in one subject—either reading or mathematics—and is given 30 minutes to respond to each block. The proposed change is to add an additional 30 minutes to the testing time for each student, for a total of 90 minutes. By increasing the testing time per student, the student sample could be reduced by a third, which would reduce administration costs, at least in the near term.

RECOMMENDATION 6-1: The National Center for Education Statistics (NCES) should continue to develop its plan to administer NAEP in longer sessions that allow for 90 minutes for the testing of cognitive items for each student. NCES should explore other models for using longer tests, in addition to its current plan. The decision to use longer tests should be based primarily on their potential to reduce testing burden by reducing the number of sampled students and to understand dependencies in proficiency across subjects, rather than being based on any long-term cost savings, which would be minimal with local test administration.

Revisiting the Sample Sizes Needed to Achieve NAEP's Purposes

Given NAEP's mission to track performance gaps, it is important that sample sizes are large enough for analyses to detect these differences. Besides simple two-way comparisons, such as differences in reading achievement across time or between Black and White students, NAEP also provides more complex multiway comparisons, such as cross tabulations that compare performance for students grouped by race, ethnicity, and gender or by race, ethnicity, gender, and family socioeconomic status, by state. The process of subdividing the full sample by multiple dimensions can create "cells" with samples sizes too small to report or make inferences about.

Reducing sample sizes is one way to reduce costs, but it needs to be done in a way that does not degrade the quality of valued comparisons and trends. Procedures called statistical power analyses are used to estimate the sample size needed to detect performance differences that are judged to be policy relevant, and they can guide NAEP in its decision making about reductions.

RECOMMENDATION 6-2: The National Center for Education Statistics should commission an analysis of the tradeoff between NAEP's sample sizes and its statistical power in detecting differences in performance, including trends and gaps, and its ability to achieve minimum cell sizes for reporting on subpopulations. In particular, this analysis should consider the stated purposes of the National Assessment Governing Board to measure not only average scores, but also differences over time and between targeted subpopulations, and it should provide evidence about the level of precision required for these results to be meaningful to educators and policy makers. Evidence about meaningful levels of statistical power and minimum cell sizes for subpopulations should be directly related to the implications for NAEP's sample sizes and associated administration costs.

Adaptive Testing

Computer-adaptive testing has been effectively used in large-scale testing since the mid-1990s. A typical adaptive test uses a student's performance on one question to assign the next question at the right level of difficulty. With each response, the computer-based algorithm updates its estimate of the student's proficiency level and selects the next question for the student to answer. Items are given to students until their proficiency can be estimated with a predetermined level of precision.

Because of the requirements of NAEP's frameworks, computer-adaptive testing at the item level and across all subscales is not practical. However, the practical problems can be addressed in multistage adaptive testing, in which the adaptation occurs over groups of items and the first stage is limited to items that can be automatically scored, though this may prevent the use of some item types and may omit consideration of some subscales in the adaptation. The coarse adaptation that is possible is unlikely to result in substantial efficiencies across the full population, but it could improve estimates for some groups.

RECOMMENDATION 6-3: The National Center for Education Statistics (NCES) should not pursue adaptive testing for NAEP as a way of saving costs, but the agency should continue to investigate its use for its potential to improve the precision of statistical estimates and the test-taking experiences for low-performing students. NCES should also consider that no single approach to adaptive testing may fit all subjects and that some changes to assessment frameworks may be necessary to facilitate adaptive administration.

Coordinating Resources with NCES's International Assessments

Coordinating the administration of one or more NAEP assessments with the administration of other NCES-administered assessments such as the Trends in International Mathematics and Science Study (TIMSS) or the Program for International Student Assessment (PISA) would potentially allow several assessment programs to share in administration costs; however, substantial difficulties would be involved. At a minimum, a coordinated approach would require that two or more assessments from different programs be administered in the same schools at the same time under roughly comparable conditions. Despite the potential cost savings, and the possibility such coordination would offer of establishing stronger statistical links across the assessments, the practical difficulties of coordination would be prohibitive and any net cost savings would be reduced as more schools are able to administer NAEP successfully with local proctors and equipment. Greater efficiencies across assessments would be possible if the content were shared or commingled, but that would entail even more practical difficulties.

RECOMMENDATION 6-4: Efforts to coordinate NAEP test administration with the international assessment programs sponsored by the National Center for Education Statistics should not be used as a strategy to reduce costs.

USING AUTOMATED ITEM SCORING

Automated scoring offers the potential to modestly reduce the cost of hand scoring NAEP's constructed-response items, with an estimated annual savings of about $1.25 million per year, which is 0.7 percent of NAEP's budget. Automated scoring is the use of statistical and computational methods to model scores assigned by human raters. Automated scoring has been widely adopted in K–12 assessment, licensure, and certification programs and is one of the most recognized applications of machine learning in educational measurement.

Automated-scoring models have displayed comparable performance relative to humans when scoring short and long essays and constructed-response items in reading comprehension and mathematics. They have also been successfully applied to mathematical expressions and equations entered using an equation editor or by graphing items using a graph interface. NAEP already has conducted proof-of-concept studies on automated scoring and, as this report was being finalized, was conducting a challenge to evaluate the performance of the latest scoring engines on reading assessment items.

The incorporation of automated scoring into NAEP would offer a number of likely benefits, including faster scoring, improved score consistency within and across administrations, higher-quality scoring of items when combined with human scoring, and increased information about student responses; it would also potentially offer cost savings. Importantly, automated scoring models do not drift and can help ensure that the scoring rubrics are applied consistently across years to support the centrality of trend to NAEP's mission. However, automated scoring models require human monitoring to examine performance, and models may need recalibration. Automated scoring also offers the potential for collecting additional diagnostic information about student responses beyond a score, with data about spelling, coherence, syntactic variation, and other linguistic features, providing more insight about student knowledge and skills.

RECOMMENDATION 7-1: The National Center for Education Statistics (NCES) should continue its work to implement automated scoring on the reading and mathematics assessments for grades 4 and 8, with the item types that current scoring engines can score accurately and consistently. NCES should also consider the use of automated scoring on other assessments administered to state-level samples. In addition to benefiting from modest net reductions in costs, NCES should work to leverage the potential of automated scoring to improve the speed of reporting, increase the information provided about open-ended responses, and increase the consistency and fairness of scoring over time.

ADOPTING INNOVATIVE ANALYSIS AND REPORTING

Arguably, all of NAEP's impact is mediated through analysis and reporting, which include not only score reports and related data and analyses, but also the frameworks, innovative example items, advanced psychometrics, and other assessment practices. NAEP score reports have regularly provided clear, high-level overviews of NAEP results. Reports that go a step further and analyze relationships between NAEP data and data from other sources are consistently among the most popular reports produced with NAEP data. Because NCES and NAGB are prohibited from using NAEP data to make policy recommendations, it is important to encourage others to use NAEP data to perform these essential analyses. Although there have been recent improvements, NCES is slow in making NAEP data available to others and the infrastructure for sharing the data is limited. The panel estimates the average annual analysis and reporting budget for NAEP at $17.6 million, which is 10.0 percent of the overall budget.

RECOMMENDATION 8-1: The National Center for Education Statistics should devote a greater percentage of its budget for innovative analysis and reporting that will increase the use and understanding of NAEP's data, including finding ways to make the raw data available more quickly to researchers, improving the usability and sophistication of the NAEP Data Explorer, making process data more easily accessible, and expanding the availability and use of important contextual variables.

DEVELOPING A NEXT-GENERATION TECHNOLOGY PLATFORM

Exploratory research in psychometrics using data science, machine learning, and artificial intelligence provides a vision of a future in which assessments are much more flexible, adaptable, and integrated into a student's learning experiences than is currently the case. To support the full range of innovations—those that should be implemented now and those that will become compelling in the next decade or even further in the future—NAEP needs a robust technology platform that is flexible enough to incorporate innovations as they become ready for application. These innovations span the full chain of the NAEP program, including test design, item and test development, test administration, analysis of results, and reporting.

NAEP currently does not have a platform with such a contemporary data architecture. Instead, NAEP data are held in separate "silos," each administered by a different Alliance contractor. This arrangement is slow and would impede efforts to implement the proposed innovations discussed in this report.

The platform and technology approach of the current eNAEP system is almost a decade old and is based in a customized application that requires dedicated tablet computers, dedicated internet routers, and technical staff at every school site in which NAEP is administered. Developing the next generation of this assessment platform is necessary to administer NAEP on local computers.

NCES and its Alliance partners are working on a new comprehensive, multicomponent system called Next-Generation "Next-Gen" eNAEP. The system will include an assessment delivery platform application for students, as well as an assessment delivery engine and an item authoring system. NCES is currently developing a system that is custom built for NAEP. However, it is possible that the new system could use existing off-the-shelf components—or components that may become available as technology advances. Given the prevalence of online testing, some components may already exist that could be used in the Next-Gen system and potentially result in cost savings.

The costs of creating an entirely new Next-Gen system are considerable, and the panel was not provided information on the costs for the planned work. The estimated average annual cost of the platform development contract is $19.2 million, which is 11.0 percent of the overall NAEP budget. In addition, the program pays $10.2 million annually for the web support contract.

RECOMMENDATION 9-1: The National Center for Education Statistics (NCES) should regularly evaluate the software built by vendors or available in open-source libraries for its potential to meet the requirements of the different components of Next-Gen eNAEP. To support the viability of local administration of NAEP, the ease of installing, managing, and troubleshooting test delivery software should be a strong consideration in selecting the software to be used. Given the substantial ongoing expense associated with developing and maintaining a proprietary platform, Next-Gen eNAEP components should be custom built only if there are clearly large net benefits from doing so that have been identified by rigorous analysis. This decision should be made on a component basis, not as a single decision to build or buy all components. NCES should immediately carry out an evaluation with respect to any components of Next-Gen eNAEP that have not already been substantially developed, and then periodically thereafter. The platform development contract should provide the right incentives to make the best decision between building and buying each component.

Next-Gen eNAEP is an ambitious enterprise software development project that requires special expertise that is not typical for many of the staff members at NCES or its contractors.

RECOMMENDATION 9-2: The National Center for Education Statistics (NCES) should ensure that there is adequate internal and external expertise related to enterprise software development to support and oversee the development of Next-Gen eNAEP for both the NCES staff and the staff working for the platform development contractor. This software expertise is substantially different than expertise related to psychometrics and statistics.

RECOMMENDATION 9-3: The National Center for Education Statistics should seek expert guidance from enterprise application developers and educational technologists who understand assessment technology platforms to evaluate the reasonability of the projected costs for the development of Next-Gen eNAEP.

TAKING A SYSTEMIC APPROACH TO DESIGNING ASSESSMENT PROGRAMS[1]

The panel estimates that management, planning, support, and oversight functions represent at least 28.7 percent of the total budget for NAEP, more than $50.3 million on average per year. This total includes costs related to federal employees and support contracts, with likely substantial additional costs for these functions in the program's non-support contracts. These costs are very large, both in absolute terms and as a percentage of the overall NAEP budget. In consequence, meaningful cost reduction for the NAEP program will need to include a consideration of potential reduction of these costs.

RECOMMENDATION 10-1: The National Assessment Governing Board and the National Center for Education Statistics should commission an independent audit of the program management and decision-making processes and costs in the NAEP program, with a charge and sufficient access to review the program's costs in detail. That audit should include proposed ways to streamline these processes.

With respect to the types of strategic innovation that are at the center of the panel's charge, the research activities that support innovation are one of the functions that is included under the label of program management, planning, support, and oversight. The absence of a coordinated structure for these activities limits the ability of the program to focus on and leverage innovation. Such research might include research related to evaluation, validity, innovative assessment items, and new assessment technologies.

RECOMMENDATION 10-2: The National Center for Education Statistics should increase the visibility and coherence of NAEP's research activities to help NAEP's stakeholders, as well as other assessment programs, understand the innovations the program is investigating and the lessons it is learning. The NAEP research program should have an identifiable budget and program of activities.

A VISION FOR THE FUTURE

NAEP has been and can continue to be an invaluable resource for the nation to understand the learning of U.S. students over time. To make that possible, however, NAEP must adapt to the evolving landscape of

[1]After a prepublication version of the report was provided to the Institute of Education Sciences, NCES, and NAGB, this section was edited to reflect a broader range of costs and to revise the description and estimate of the costs associated with the non-support contracts.

technology and be mindful of the costs of its past practices and upcoming decisions. The analysis and recommendations in this report are offered as a way for NAEP to evolve to serve its important purposes for policy makers and the public well into the 2030s.

References

AASA. (2021, September). *School District Spending of American Rescue Plan Funding*. Available: https://aasa.org/uploadedFiles/ARP-Survey-Findings-090121.pdf.

American Educational Research Association, American Psychological Association, and National Council on Measurement in Education. (2014). *Standards for Educational and Psychological Testing*. Washington, DC: American Educational Research Association.

Beaton, A.E. (1990). Epilogue. In A.E. Beaton and R. Zwick (Eds.), *The Effect of Changes in the National Assessment: Disentangling the NAEP 1985-1986 Reading Anomaly* (pp. 165–168). Princeton, NJ: Educational Testing Service.

Beaton, A.E., Barone, J.L., Campbell, A., Ferris, JJ., Freund, D.S., Johnson, E.G., Johnson, J.R., Kaplan, B.A., Kline, D.L., MacDonald, W., Mead, N.A., Mislevy, R.J., Mullis, I.V.S., Narcowich, M.A., Norris, N.A., Rogers, A.M., Sheehan, K.M., Yamamoto, K., Zwick, R., Braden, J., Burke, J., Caldwell, N, Hansen, M.H., Lago, J.A., Rust, K., Slobasky, R., and Tepping, B.J. (1988). *The NAEP 1985-86 Technical Report*. Educational Testing Service. Available: https://eric.ed.gov/?id=ED355248.

Bejar, I.I. (2011, August). A validity-based approach to quality control and assurance of automated scoring. *Assessment in Education: Principles, Policy & Practice*, *18*(3), 319–341.

Bejar, I.I. (2019). *ASVAB AIG (WK, AR, MK, and GS) in Minutes of the Defense Advisory Committee on Military Personnel Testing: September 26-27, 2019 Meeting*. Available: https://dacmpt.com/wp-content/uploads/2020/04/Full-DACMPT-Meeting-Minutes-Sep-2019-FINAL.pdf.

Bennett, R. (2011). *Automated Scoring of Constructed-Response Literacy and Mathematics Items*. Available: https://www.researchgate.net/publication/260346149_Automated_Scoring_of_Constructed-Response_Literacy_and_Mathematics_Items.

Bergner, Y., and von Davier, A.A. (2019). Process data in NAEP: Past, present, and future. *Journal of Educational and Behavioral Statistics*, *44*(6), 706–732. Available: https://doi.org/10.3102/1076998618784700.

Bridgeman, B., Trapani, C., and Attali, Y. (2012). Comparison of human and machine scoring of essays: Differences by gender, ethnicity, and country. *Applied Measurement in Education*, *25*(1), 27–40. Available: https://doi.org/10.1080/08957347.2012.635502.

Brown, G. (2019). Technologies and infrastructure: Costs and obstacles in developing large-scale computer-based testing. *Education Inquiry*, *10*(1), 4–20. Available: https://doi.org/10.1080/20004508.2018.1529528.

Burstein, J., and Chodorow, M. (1999, June). Automated essay scoring for nonnative English speakers. In *Proceedings of the ACL99 Workshop on Computer-Mediated Language Assessment and Evaluation of Natural Language Processing*. College Park, MD.

Cahill, A., Fife, J., Riordan, B., Vajpayee, A., and Galochkin, D. (2020). Context-based automated scoring of complex mathematics responses. In *Proceedings of the 15th Workshop on Innovative Use of NLP for Building Educational Applications*. Seattle, WA.

Center for Process Data. (n.d.). *American Institutes for Research*. Available: https://www.air.org/project/center-process-data.

Chingos, M.M. (2012, November). *Strength in Numbers: State Spending on K-12 Assessment Systems*. Brown Center on Education Policy at Brookings. Available: https://www.brookings.edu/wp-content/uploads/2016/06/11_assessment_chingos_final_new.pdf.

Circi, R., Sikali, E., Sahin, F., Zheng, X., Hicks, J., Youn Lee, S., and Caliço, T.A. (2020, June 10). *The Future is Here: Analyzing NAEP Process Data Using R*. American Educational Research Association Virtual Research Learning Series. Available: https://www.aera.net/Professional-Opportunities-Funding/AERA-Virtual-Research-Learning-Series2020.

Corbett-Davies, S., and Goel, S. (2018). The measure and mismeasure of fairness: A critical review of fair machine learning. *Cornell University ArXiv*. Available: https://arxiv.org/abs/1808.00023.

DiCerbo, K., Lai, E., and Ventura, M. (2020). Assessment design with automated scoring in mind. In A. Rupp, P. Foltz, and D. Yi (Eds.), *Handbook of Automated Scoring*. Boca Raton, FL: CRC Press.

Embretson, S.E., and Kingston, N.M. (2018). Automatic item generation: A more efficient process for developing mathematics achievement items? *Journal of Educational Measurement*, *55*(1), 112–131. Available: https://doi.org/10.1111/jedm.12166.

Ferrara, S., Lai, E., Reilly, A., and Nichols, P.D. (2017). Principled approaches to assessment design, development and implementation. In A.A. Rupp and J.P. Leighton (Eds.), *The Handbook of Cognition and Assessment, Frameworks, Methodologies and Applications* (pp. 41–74). West Sussex, UK: Wiley.

Fife, J. H. (2017). *The M-Rater™ Engine: Introduction to the Automated Scoring of Mathematics Items* (Research Memorandum No. RM-17-02). Princeton, NJ: Educational Testing Service.

Foltz, P., Yan, D., and Rupp, A. (2020). The past, present, and future of automated scoring. In A. Rupp, P. Foltz, and D. Yi (Eds.), *Handbook of Automated Scoring*. Boca Raton, FL: CRC Press.

Ghosh, D., Klebanov, B., and Song, Y. (2020, April). An exploratory study of argumentative writing by young students: A transformer-based approach. In *Proceedings of the 15th Workshop on Innovative Use of NLP for Building Educational Applications*. Seattle, WA.

Gierl, M.J., and Haladyna, T.M. (2013). *Automatic Item Generation: Theory and Practice*. New York: Routledge.

Glaser, R., Linn, R., and Bohrnstedt, G. (1997). *Assessments in Transition: Monitoring the Nation's Educational Progress*. Stanford, CA: National Academy of Education.

Haertel, E. (2016). *Future of NAEP Long-Term Trend Assessments*. A white paper prepared for the National Assessment Governing Board. Available: https://www.nagb.gov/content/dam/nagb/en/documents/newsroom/naep-releases/naep-long-term-trend-symposium/long-term-trends.pdf.

Herold, B. (2016, February 3). PARCC Scores lower for students who took exams on computers: Discrepancy raises questions about fairness. *Education Week*. Available: https://www.edweek.org/teaching-learning/parcc-scores-lower-for-students-who-took-exams-on-computers/2016/02.

Hoagwood, K.E., Olin, S.S., Storfer-Isser, A., Kuppinger, A., Shorter, P., Wang, N.M., Pollock, M., Peth-Pierce, R., and Horwitz, S. (2018). Evaluation of a train-the-trainers model for family peer advocates in children's mental health. *Journal of Child and Family Studies*, *27*(4), 1130–1136. Available: http://dx.doi.org.library.capella.edu/10.1007/s10826-017-0961-8.

Hutchinson, B., and Mitchell, M. (2019, January). 50 years of test (un)fairness: Lessons for machine learning. In *FAT* '19: Conference on Fairness, Accountability and Transparency*. Atlanta, GA.

Irvine, S.H. (2002). Introduction. In S.H. Irvine and P.C. Kyllonen (Eds.), *Item Generation for Test Development*. New York: Routledge.

Irvine, S.H. (2014). *Computerised Test Generation for Cross-National Military Recruitment: A Handbook*. Amsterdam: IOS Press.

Jacobson, L. (2021, August 6). Board overseeing Nation's Report Card moves past equity dispute, adopting 'forward-looking' plan for new reading tests. *T74 Newsletter*. Available: https://www.the74million.org/board-overseeing-nations-report-card-moves-past-equity-dispute-adopting-forward-looking-plan-for-new-reading-tests.

Kosh, A.E., Simpson, M.A., Bickel, L., Kellogg, M., and Sanford-Moore, E. (2019). A cost–benefit analysis of automatic item generation. *Educational Measurement: Issues and Practice*, *38*(1), 48–53. Available: https://doi.org/10.1111/emip.12237.

Leacock, C., and Zhang, X. (2014, April). *Identifying Predictors of Machine/Human Reliability for Short Response Items*. Paper presented at the annual conference of the National Council on Measurement in Education. Philadelphia, PA.

Leacock, C., Messineo, D., and Zhang, X. (2013, April). *Issues in Prompt Selection for Automated Scoring of Short Answer Questions*. Paper presented at the annual conference of the National Council on Measurement in Education. San Francisco, CA.

Lockee, B.B. (2021). Shifting digital, shifting context: (Re)considering teacher professional development for online and blended learning in the COVID-19 era. *Educational Technology Research and Development*, *69*, 17–20. Available: https://link.springer.com/article/10.1007/s11423-020-09836-8.

Lord, F.M. (1980). *Applications of Item Response Theory to Practical Testing Problems*. Mahwah, NJ: Erlbaum.

Lottridge, S., Burkhardt, A., and Boyer, M. (2020). Automated scoring [Digital ITEMS Module 18]. *Educational Measurement: Issues and Practice*, *39*(3).

Lottridge, S., Wood, S., and Shaw, D. (2018). The effectiveness of score-ability ratings in predicting automated scoring performance. *Applied Measurement in Education*, *31*(3), 215–232.

Luecht, R.M. (2005). Some useful cost-benefit criteria for evaluating computer-based test delivery models and systems. *Journal of Applied Testing Technology*, *7*(2). Available: www.testpublishers.org/journal.htm.

———. (2006). Operational issues in computer-based testing. In D. Bartrum and R.K. Hambleton (Eds.), *Computer-based Testing and the Internet: Issues and Advances* (pp. 39–58). New York: Wiley and Sons.

———. (2012a). An introduction to assessment engineering for automatic item generation. In M. Gierl and T. Haladyna (Eds.), *Automatic Item Generation* (pp. 59–101). New York: Taylor & Francis/Routledge.

———. (2012b). Automatic item generation for computerized adaptive testing. In M. Gierl and T. Haladyna (Eds.), *Automatic Item Generation* (pp. 196–216). New York: Taylor & Francis/Routledge.

———. (2014). Computerized adaptive multistage design considerations and operational issues. In D. Yan, A. A. von Davier, and C. Lewis (Eds.), *Computerized Multistage Testing: Theory and Applications* (pp. 69–83). London, UK: CRC Press/Taylor & Francis Group.

———. (2016). Computer-based test delivery models, data and operational implementation issues. In F. Drasgow (Ed.), *Testing and Technology: Improving Educational and Psychological Measurement* (pp. 179–205). New York: Routledge.

———. (2020a). Generating performance-level descriptors under a principled assessment design paradigm: An example for assessments under the Next-Generation Science Standards. *Educational Measurement Issues and Practice*, *39*(4), 105–115.

———. (2020b). *The Challenges of Principled Item Design*. NCME symposium, Principled item design: State-of-the-art symposium paper for the Annual Meeting of the National Council on Measurement in Education. Online.

Luecht, R., and Burke, M. (2020). Reconceptualizing items: From clones and automatic item generation to task model families. In R. Lissitz and H. Jiao (Eds.), *Applications of Artificial Intelligence to Assessment* (pp. 25–49). Baltimore, MD: Information Age Publishers.

Markowetz, A., Błaszkiewicz, K., Montag, C., Switala, C., and Schlaepfer, T.E. (2014). Psycho-informatics: Big data shaping modern psychometrics. *Medical Hypotheses*, *82*(4), 405–411. Available: https://doi.org/10.1016/j.mehy.2013.11.030.

Mathias, S., and Bhattacharyya, P. (2020, April). *Can Neural Networks Automatically Score Essay Traits?* 15th Workshop on Innovative Use of NLP for Building Educational Applications. Seattle, WA.

McGraw-Hill Education CTB. (2014, December 24). *Smarter Balanced Assessment Consortium Field Test: Automated Scoring Research Studies* (in accordance with Smarter Balanced RFP 17). Available: http://www.smarterapp.org/documents/FieldTest_AutomatedScoringResearchStudies.pdf.

Michel, R. (2021). Remotely proctored K-12 high stakes standardized testing during COVID-19: Will it last? *Educational Measurement: Issues and Practice*, *39*(3), 28–30.

Mislevy, R.J. (2006). Cognitive psychology and educational assessment. In R.L. Brennan (Ed.), *Educational Measurement*, 4th ed. (pp. 257–306). Washington, DC: American Council on Education.

———. (2019). On integrating psychometrics and learning analytics in complex assessments. *Data Analytics and Psychometrics: Informing Assessment Practices*, 1–52.

Mislevy, R.J., Steinberg, L.S., and Almond, R.G. (2003). On the structure of educational assessments. *Measurement: Interdisciplinary Research and Perspectives*, *1*, 3–66.

Mosquin, P., and Chromy, J. (2004). *Federal Sample Sizes for Confirmation of State Tests in the No Child Left Behind Act.* Commissioned by the NAEP Validity Studies Panel. Available: https://www.air.org/resource/report/federal-sample-sizes-confirmation-state-tests-no-child-left-behind-act.

NAEP (National Assessment of Educational Progress). (2013). *NAEP Technical Documentation: NAEP Scoring*. Available: https://nces.ed.gov/nationsreportcard/tdw/scoring.

NAGB (National Assessment Governing Board). (1996, August 2). *Redesigning the National Assessment of Educational Progress*. Available: https://www.air.org/resource/report/federal-sample-sizes-confirmation-state-tests-no-child-left-behind-act.

———. (2017, May 19–20). *Official Summary of Governing Board Actions*. Available: https://www.nagb.gov/content/dam/nagb/en/documents/what-we-do/quarterly-board-meeting-materials/2017-08/02-may-2017-board-meeting-minutes.pdf.

———. (2018, March 3). *Framework Development Policy Statement*. Available: https://www.nagb.gov/content/dam/nagb/en/documents/policies/framework-development.pdf.

———. (2019a, November 15). Strategic vision activities led by COSDAM. In *Committee on Standards, Design and Methodology Agenda* (p. 3). Available: https://www.nagb.gov/content/dam/nagb/en/documents/what-we-do/quarterly-board-meeting-materials/2019-11/05-committee-on-standards-design-and-methodology.pdf.

———. (2019b). *Reading Framework for the 2019 National Assessment of Educational Progress*. U.S. Department of Education. Available: https://files.eric.ed.gov/fulltext/ED604485.pdf.

———. (2021, August 5). *National Assessment of Educational Progress Schedule of Assessments*. Available: https://www.nagb.gov/content/dam/nagb/en/documents/naep/Schedule%20of%20Assessments_080521.pdf.

NASEM (National Academies of Sciences, Engineering, and Medicine). (2017). *Evaluation of the Achievement Levels for Mathematics and Reading on the National Assessment of Educational Progress*. Washington, DC: The National Academies Press.

Nation's Report Card. (n.d.). *Response Process Data from the 2017 NAEP Grade 8. Mathematics Assessment*. Available: https://www.nationsreportcard.gov/process_data.

NCES (National Center for Educational Statistics). (2012). *NAEP: Looking Ahead—Leading Assessments into the Future*. Washington, DC: NCES.

———. (2013). *The Nation's Report Card: Trends in Academic Progress 2012* (NCES 2013 456). Washington, DC: Institute of Education Sciences, U.S. Department of Education.

NGSS Lead States (Next Generation Science Standards Lead States). (2013). *Next Generation Science Standards: For States, By States*. Washington, DC: The National Academies Press.

O'Malley, F., and Norton, S. (2022). *Maintaining the Validity of the NAEP Frameworks and Assessments in Civics and U.S. History*. Commissioned by the NAEP Validity Studies Panel. Washington, DC: American Institutes for Research.

Oranje, A., Mazzeo, J., Xu, X., and Kulick, E. (2014). A multistage approach to group-score assessments. In D. Yan, A. van Davier, and C. Lewis (Eds.), *Computerized Multistage Testing; Theory and Applications*. New York: Routledge.

Page, E. (2003). Project Essay Grade. In *Automated Essay Scoring: A Cross-Disciplinary Perspective* (pp. 43–54). Mahwah, NJ: Lawrence Erlbaum Associates.

Partnership for Assessment of Readiness for College and Careers. (2015, March 9). *Research Results of PARCC Automated Scoring Proof of Concept Study*.

Patz, R., Lottridge, S., and Boyer, M. (2019, April). *Human Rating Errors and the Training of Automated Raters*. Paper presented at the National Council on Measurement in Education. Toronto, CA.

Provasnik, S. (2021). Process data, the new frontier for assessment development: Rich new soil or a quixotic quest? *Large-Scale Assessments in Education*, *9*(1), 1. Available: https://doi.org/10.1186/s40536-020-00092-z.

Raczynski, K., Choi, H-J., and Cohen, A. (2021, June). *Using Latent Class Analysis to Explore the AI Score-Ability of Constructed-Response Items*. Paper presented at the National Council on Measurement in Education (NCME). Online.

Ramineni, C., and Williamson, D. (2018). Understanding mean score differences between the e-rater® automated scoring engine and humans for demographically based groups in the GRE® general test. *ETS Research Report Series*, *2018*(1), 1–31.

Riordan, B., Bichler, S., Bradford, A., Chen, J., Wily, K., Gerard, L, and Linn, M. (2020, April). *An Empirical Investigation of Neural Methods for Content Scoring of Science Explanations*. 15th Workshop on Innovative Use of NLP for Building Educational Applications. Seattle, WA.

Roll, I., and Winne, P.H. (2015). Understanding, evaluating, and supporting self-regulated learning using learning analytics. *Journal of Learning Analytics*, *2*(1), 7–12. Available: https://doi.org/10.18608/jla.2015.21.2.

Romero, C., and Ventura, S. (2020). Educational data mining and learning analytics: An updated survey. *WIREs Data Mining and Knowledge Discovery*, *10*(3), e1355. Available: https://doi.org/10.1002/widm.1355.

Rudner, L.M. (2010). Implementing the Graduate Management Admission Test computerized adaptive test. Chapter 8 in W.J. van der Linden and C.A.W. Glas, eds., *Elements of Adaptive Testing*. New York: Springer. Availabile: https://link.springer.com/content/pdf/10.1007/978-0-387-85461-8.pdf.

Shermis, M., and Hamner, B. (2013). Contrasting state-of-the-art automated scoring of essay: Analysis. In *The Handbook of Automated Essay Evaluation: Current Applications and New Directions* (pp. 313–346). New York: Routledge Academic.

Shermis, M., and, Lottridge, S. (2019, April). *Communicating to the Public about Machine Scoring: What Works, What Doesn't*. Paper presented at the National Council on Measurement in Education. Toronto, CA.

Shermis, M., Mao, L., Mulholland, M., and Kieftenbeld, V. (2017). Use of automated scoring features to generate hypothesis regarding language-based DIF. *International Journal of Testing*, *17*(5), 1–21.

Steiber, A. (2014). *The Google Model: Managing Continuous Innovation in a Rapidly Changing World*. Switzerland: Springer International.

Strauss, V. (2020, May 30). Testing giants ACT and college board struggle amid COVID-19 pandemic. *Washington Post*. Available: https://www.washingtonpost.com/education/2020/05/30/testing-giants-act-college-board-struggle-amid-covid-19-pandemic.

Swain, M., Wise, L., and Kroopnick, M. (2018). *Feasibility of a Multi-Stage Testing Design*. Presentation at NCME (NYC), in the session on Maintaining Quality Assessments in the Face of Change.

Topol, B., Olson, J., and Roeber, E. (2014, February). *Pricing Study: Machine Scoring of Student Essays*. Available: https://www.gettingsmart.com/wp-content/uploads/2014/02/ASAP-Pricing-Study-Final.pdf.

Ul Hassan, M., and Miller, F. (2019). Optimal item calibration for computerized achievement tests. *Psychometrika*, *84*, 1101–1128. Available: https://doi.org/10.1007/s11336-019-09673-6.

van der Linden, W.J., and Pashley, P.J. (2010). Item selection and ability estimation adaptive testing. In W.J. van der Linden and C.A.W. Glas (Eds.), *Elements of Adaptive Testing* (pp. 3–30). New York, NY: Springer.

Verschoor A., Berger S., Moser U., and Kleintjes, F. (2019). On-the-fly calibration in computerized adaptive testing. In B. Veldkamp and C. Sluijter (Eds.), *Theoretical and Practical Advances in Computer-Based Educational Measurement: Methodology of Educational Measurement and Assessment*. Cham: Springer. Available: https://doi.org/10.1007/978-3-030-18480-3_16.

von Davier, A.A., Deonovic, B., Yudelson, M., Polyak, S.T., and Woo, A. (2019). Computational psychometrics approach to holistic learning and assessment systems. *Frontiers in Education*, *4*, 69. Available: https://doi.org/10.3389/feduc.2019.00069.

Wang, X., Talluri, S.T., Rose, C., and Koedinger, K. (2019). UpGrade: Sourcing student open-ended solutions to create scalable learning opportunities. In *L@S '19: Proceedings of the Sixth (2019) ACM Conference on Learning @ Scale*, Article 17. https://doi.org/10.1145/3330430.3333614.

Way, D., and Strain-Seymour, E. (2021). *A Framework for Considering Device and Interface Features that May Affect Student Performance on the National Assessment of Educational Progress*. White paper commissioned by the NAEP Validity Studies (NVS) Panel. Available: https://www.air.org/resource/report/framework-considering-device-and-interface-features-may-affect-student-performance.

Williamson, D., Xi, X., and Breyer, F.J. (2012). A framework for the evaluation and use of automated scoring. *Educational Measurement: Issues and Practice*, *31*(1), 2–13.

Wind, W., Wolfe, E., Engelhard, G., and Foltz, P. (2017). The influence of rater effects in training sets on the psychometric quality of automated scoring for writing assessments. *International Journal of Testing*, *18*(1), 1–23.

Winter, P. C., Karvonen, M., and Christensen, L. L. (2018, August). Developing item templates for alternate assessments of English language proficiency. Madison, WI: University of Wisconsin–Madison, Alternate English Language Learning Assessment (ALTELLA). Available: http://altella.wceruw.org/resources.html.

Wood, S. (2020). Public perception and communication around automated essay scoring. In A. Rupp, P. Foltz, and D. Yi (Eds.), *Handbook of Automated Scoring: Theory into Practice*. Boca Raton, FL: CRC Press.

Yan, D., and Bridgeman, B. (2020). Validation of automated scoring systems. In D. Yan, A. Rupp, and P. Foltz (Eds.), *Handbook of Automated Scoring: Theory into Practice*. Boca Raton, FL: CRC Press.

Young, T., Hazarika, D., Poria, S., and Cambria, E. (2017). *Recent Trends in Deep Learning Based Natural Language Processing*. Available: https://arxiv.org/pdf/1708.02709.pdf.

Appendix A

Biographical Sketches of Panel Members and Staff

KAREN J. MITCHELL (*Chair*) recently retired as senior director of the Medical College Admission Test (MCAT) at the Association of American Medical Colleges (AAMC). At AAMC, Mitchell oversaw test development and scoring, test administration and reporting, test preparation services, testing research, and outreach and communication. She directed the redesign and 2015 launch of the current version of the MCAT exam and directed its continued administration during COVID-19. Previously, at the RAND Corporation and U.S. Army Research Institute for the Behavioral and Social Sciences, she directed research on the validity and use of large-scale accountability and selection tests. As a senior program officer at the National Research Council, she directed research on the role of licensure tests in improving teacher quality, codirected the congressionally mandated evaluation of NAEP, and worked on the evaluation of the Voluntary National Tests. She has a Ph.D. in educational research methodology from Cornell University.

ISAAC I. BEJAR recently retired from the Educational Testing Service, where he held the position of principal research scientist. For most of his career, his research focused on the application of technology and cognitive science to the scoring of constructed responses, adaptive testing, and automated item generation (AIG). With funding from the Department of Defense, he is currently carrying out research on AIG in the context of the Armed Services Vocational Aptitude Battery. He has authored multiple journal articles, chapters, and books on these topics, and holds several patents related to human and automated scoring. He has a Ph.D. in psychology from the University of Minnesota.

SEAN PATRICK (JACK) BUCKLEY is head of assessment and learning sciences at Roblox. Previously, he was president and chief scientist at Imbellus, a game-based assessment technology startup. He also previously served as senior vice president at the American Institutes for Research (AIR), where he led the research and evaluation area, and he still serves as an AIR fellow on several projects, including chairing the NAEP Validity Studies Panel. Before joining AIR, he helped lead the redesign of the Scholastic Aptitude Test (SAT) at the College Board, where he served as senior vice president of research. Earlier, he served as commissioner of the U.S. Department of Education's NCES, where he was responsible for the measurement of all aspects of U.S. education, including conducting the National Assessment of Educational Progress and coordinating participation in international assessments. He has a Ph.D. in political science from SUNY Stony Brook.

STUART W. ELLIOTT (*Study Director*) is a scholar in the Division of Behavioral and Social Sciences and Education of the National Academies of Sciences, Engineering, and Medicine. Previously at the National Academies, as the director of the Board on Testing and Assessment, he led numerous studies on educational tests and indicators, assessment of science and 21st-century skills, applications of information technology, and occupational preparation and certification. He recently spent 3 years at the Organisation for Economic Co-operation and Development (OECD) working with their test of adult skills, resulting in a 2017 report, *Computers and the Future of Skill Demand.* He has a B.A. in economics from Columbia University and a Ph.D. in economics from the Massachusetts Institute of Technology, and he received postdoctoral training in cognitive psychology at Carnegie Mellon University.

BRIAN GONG is senior associate and cofounder of the Center for Assessment, a nonprofit organization that provides technical assistance around assessment and accountability primarily to states, districts, and related organizations, including the Council of Chief State School Officers and the U.S. Department of Education. He provides wide-ranging knowledge of innovations in large-scale assessment—including computer-assisted testing, online test administration, automated scoring, performance assessment, innovative item types—as well as of the challenges of making such innovations operationally feasible and legally defensible, including accommodations and supports for the full range of students with disabilities. He has served on many committees, including the committee responsible for the most recent edition of the *Standards for Educational and Psychological*

Testing, the Validation Committee for the *Common Core State Standards*, the group that produced *Initiative on the Future of NAEP* for the National Center for Education Statistics, and the NAEP Quality Assurance Technical Panel. He has a Ph.D. in education from Stanford.

ANDREW D. HO is Charles William Eliot professor of education at the Harvard Graduate School of Education. He is a psychometrician whose research aims to improve the design, use, and interpretation of test scores in educational policy and practice. He is director of the National Council on Measurement in Education and a trustee for the Carnegie Foundation for the Advancement of Teaching. He served two terms as a member of the National Assessment Governing Board, where he chaired the Committee on Standards, Design, and Methodology. He also chaired the research committee for the vice provost for advances in learning at Harvard University, which governed research on "massive" open online courses. He is an elected member of the National Academy of Education. He has a Ph.D. in educational psychology from Stanford.

JUDITH KOENIG (*Senior Program Officer*) is on the staff of the Committee on National Statistics of the National Academies of Science, Engineering, and Medicine, where she directs measurement-related studies designed to inform education policy. Her work has included studies on the National Assessment of Educational Progress; teacher licensure and advanced-level certification; inclusion of special-needs students and English-language learners in assessment programs; setting standards for the National Assessment of Adult Literacy; assessing 21st-century skills; and using value-added methods for evaluating schools and teachers. Previously, she worked at the Association of American Medical Colleges and as a special education teacher and diagnostician. She has a B.A. in elementary and special education from Michigan State University, an M.A. in psychology from George Mason University, and a Ph.D. in educational measurement, statistics, and evaluation from the University of Maryland.

STEPHEN LAZER is president and CEO of Questar Assessment, Incorporated. Previously, he served held various positions at Educational Testing Service (ETS), where he served as NAEP social studies coordinator, NAEP development director, NAEP executive director, and cognizant corporate officer for NAEP. At ETS he also served as vice president of assessment development from and as senior vice president for student and teacher assessment. He has written extensively on NAEP and has served as a resource to previous studies of the program. He has a B.A. degree in political science and English from McGill University and an M.A. degree in political science from Princeton.

SUSAN MARIE LOTTRIDGE is senior director of automated scoring at Cambium Assessment, Inc. (CAI). In this role, she leads CAI's machine learning and scoring team on the research, development, and operation of CAI's automated scoring software. This software includes automated essay scoring, short-answer scoring, automated speech scoring, and an engine that detects disturbing content in student responses. In this and previous work, she has contributed to the design, research, and use of multiple automated scoring engines including equation scoring, essay scoring, short answer scoring, alert detection, and dialogue systems. She has a Ph.D. in assessment and measurement from James Madison University.

RICHARD M. LUECHT is professor of educational research methodology at the University of North Carolina at Greensboro, where he teaches graduate courses in applied statistics and advanced measurement topics, including advanced item response theory modeling and estimation, computer-based testing systems and methods, and test score equating. His research and expertise include the integration of statistical, computer science, and cognitive science technologies in assessment, advanced psychometric modeling and estimation, and the application of industrial engineering design principles to the design and construction of test (i.e., the "assessment engineering" framework). He has designed numerous algorithms and software programs for automated test assembly and devised a comprehensive computerized adaptive multistage testing framework used by several large-scale testing programs. He is also a technical consultant and advisor for many state departments of education and large-scale testing organizations. He has a Ph.D. in educational psychology, statistics, and measurement from the University of Wisconsin-Milwaukee.

ROCHELLE S. MICHEL is senior proposal writer and the state team lead on the bids and proposals team at Curriculum Associates. She has held a number of positions in the areas of educational testing, assessment, educational research, and nonprofit program management, including executive director of admission programs at Educational Records Bureau; director of research in the Academic to Career Research Center at Educational Testing Service (ETS); research director at Curriculum Associates; and psychometric manager at ETS. She is a member of the American Psychological Association, the National Council on Measurement in Education (NCME), and the Northeastern Educational Research Association, and she currently serves on the editorial boards of *NCME Applications of Educational Measurement and Assessment*, a book series, and NCME's journal, *Educational Measurement: Issues and Practice*. She is a past president of the Northeastern Educational Research Association. She has a Ph.D. in psychometrics from Fordham University.

SCOTT NORTON is deputy executive director of programs at the Council of Chief State School Officers (CCSSO). In this role, he oversees the programmatic work of the council, including student expectations, student transitions, teacher workforce, and school leadership/school improvement. He previously held the position of strategic initiative director for standards, assessment, and accountability at CCSSO. Prior to joining CCSSO, he worked as the assistant superintendent of the Office of Standards, Assessments, and Accountability at the Louisiana Department of Education, and as a public school teacher in Louisiana. He is continuing long-time service as a member of the NAEP Validity Studies Panel. He has a Ph.D. in educational administration and supervision from Louisiana State University.

JOHN WHITMER is senior fellow in data science with the Federation of American Scientists. In this position, he works on activities to implement data science into operational programs, expand data access and usability, and support the creation of an ongoing data science fellowship program at the Institute of Education Sciences at the U.S. Department of Education. Previously, he led teams of data scientists, research scientists, and machine learning engineers in large educational assessment companies (ACTNext), edTech providers (Blackboard), and educational institutions (California State University and California Community Colleges). An educational researcher by training, he approaches these projects with a commitment to improving the lives of underserved and marginalized students through advanced computational methods. He has an Ed.D. in educational leadership from the University of California-Davis.

Appendix B

Disclosure of Unavoidable Conflict of Interest

The conflict of interest policy of the National Academies of Sciences, Engineering, and Medicine[1] prohibits the appointment of an individual to a committee authoring a Consensus Study Report if the individual has a conflict of interest that is relevant to the task to be performed. An exception to this prohibition is permitted if the National Academies determines that the conflict is unavoidable and the conflict is publicly disclosed. A determination of a conflict of interest for an individual is not an assessment of that individual's actual behavior or character or ability to act objectively despite the conflicting interest.

Under institutional policy, Stephen Lazer has a conflict of interest in relation to his service on the committee on Opportunities for NAEP in an Age of AI and Pervasive Computation: A Pragmatic Vision for 2030 and Beyond. This conflict exists because, as president and CEO of Questar Assessment, Lazer works for a company that is a wholly owned, independently operated subsidiary of ETS, the lead contractor for the NAEP program.

The National Academies has concluded that in order for the committee to accomplish the tasks for which it was established, it must include a committee member with current experience in large-scale assessment programs and extensive knowledge of the structural constraints of the NAEP program. As his biographical sketch makes clear, Lazer led key parts of the NAEP work at ETS for two decades, which gave him a detailed understanding of the constraints and tradeoffs that are inherent to the program. At the same time, he has a decade of recent experience in other large-scale

[1] See http://www.nationalacademies.org/coi.

assessment programs in education that have addressed the practicality of a wide range of potential innovations and also provide him with the necessary breadth and independence which will be invaluable to assessing innovations for NAEP. His combined knowledge of the structural constraints of NAEP and the range of innovations implemented in other large-scale assessment programs will be critical to understanding the potential value for the NAEP program of the innovations the study will consider.

The National Academies has determined that the experience and expertise of Lazer is needed for the committee to accomplish the task for which it has been established. The National Academies could not find another available individual with the equivalent expertise and breadth of experience who does not have a conflict of interest under institutional policy. Therefore, the National Academies has concluded that the conflict is unavoidable.

The National Academies believes that Lazer can serve effectively as a member of the committee, and the committee can produce an objective report, taking into account the composition of the committee, the work to be performed, and the procedures to be followed in completing the study.

COMMITTEE ON NATIONAL STATISTICS

The Committee on National Statistics was established in 1972 at the National Academies of Sciences, Engineering, and Medicine to improve the statistical methods and information on which public policy decisions are based. The committee carries out studies, workshops, and other activities to foster better measures and fuller understanding of the economy, the environment, public health, crime, education, immigration, poverty, welfare, and other public policy issues. It also evaluates ongoing statistical programs and tracks the statistical policy and coordinating activities of the federal government, serving a unique role at the intersection of statistics and public policy. The committee's work is supported by a consortium of federal agencies through a National Science Foundation grant, a National Agricultural Statistics Service cooperative agreement, and several individual contracts.